Ron's respectful attitude and excellent listening years of experience and practical advice makes him unique. In a world where self-promotion often substitutes for substance, Ron is the real deal. It is a joy to work with him.

— Phyllis Zahnd, Ph.D.
Academic Organizing and Time Management

Ron Katz provided sound and practical advice on everything from writing a resume to interviewing and presentations. As someone who had worked in the same organization for 30 years, I needed the perspective of a top-notch professional job coach.

— Marcia M. Brewster
Senior Consultant and Technical Editor

Ron gave me the courage to reinvent myself for a new stage of my life and to return to a previous career, which I had loved.

— Theresa DeLise
Academic Librarian

Ron has helped me identify my weaknesses, propped me up and made me feel confident before a big interview, and always, no matter how much anxiety or angst, Ron has been able to make me laugh at the world we inhabit. He knows how to give a person who is hurting time and space, and he is aware of process. And most importantly, Ron has taught me "you can always start over."

— Emma Fessler, LCSWR

Ron Katz has the rare talent of identifying and then marketing the knowledge, problem solving, or physical skill one has that others will buy.

— Bill Hladky
Audit Professional

As a college graduate entering today's professional landscape without a compass, I found that Ron's insights put my skills into practical context. His advice proves invaluable time and time again.

— Andrew Grossman

SOMEONE'S GONNA GET HIRED...

IT MIGHT AS WELL BE YOU!

Published by PHRC
New Rochelle, New York

Back cover photo by www.ArnoldAdler.com
Excerpt from "Some Kind of Hero" by David Roth used
with permission of David Roth/MaytheLightMusic (ASCAP)
copyright 1994. Visit www.DavidRothMusic.com

ISBN: 978-0-578-05728-6

Printed in the United States of America

SOMEONE'S GONNA GET HIRED...

IT MIGHT AS WELL BE YOU!

RONALD M. KATZ

PHRC
New York

For Rita,
who has the hardest job.
Without her I am nothing,
and with her,
I have everything.

ACKNOWLEDGEMENTS

No book is the sole product of one person and least of all a book like this. First and foremost I wish to thank all the people who have attended meetings of the Job Support Group at the First Unitarian Society of Westchester in Hastings-on-Hudson, NY. Many of the stories in this book are yours. The disappointments, the anxiety and the triumphs. Over the years you have helped one another, held one another and celebrated whenever someone "brought the donuts" signaling that they had landed. By sharing so generously of yourselves you have shepherded each other through the hard times and now you offer that support to countless others. This book would not exist if not for all of you, whether you attended just a few meetings or a few months. Most notably I wish to thank Phyllis Zahnd, Emma Fessler, Peter Kassan, Ken Lee, and Helen Bird. I would also like to thank Reverend David Bryce, who first asked me to create the group to assist members of the congregation and was instrumental in its formation.

Carter Smith, the book's project director and editor, and Irene Ledwith, my art director, were the first people to whom I was not related who got to read this manuscript. I am indebted to them for their enthusiasm, guidance and the contribution of their immense talents. Also, many thanks to copy editor Ingrid Accardi and indexer Diane Brenner.

Colleagues who have shared ideas with me and supported me include Tom Willett, Tony Panos, Mary Rudder, Michael Goodman, and Tom Terez. Dear friends, as well as colleagues, Karin Levitt, John Colon, Kevin Durkin and David Roth were instrumental in providing insights, ideas and encouragement.

Thanks to Max Rodriguez and the New Rochelle Public Library for guidance and support in how to progress from an idea to a manuscript to getting published. Todd Raphael was one of the first people to encourage me to write and then edited many of my earliest attempts with care and precision. For his advice in those fragile times and the opportunities he presented, I am most grateful. Sam Horn's excellent webinars helped me believe that I had something of value to say, and that someone might benefit from my saying it.

On a more personal level, I wish to acknowledge my father, Albert Katz, who gave me some of my first lessons about the workplace and for years has said, "Write the book!" Dad, here it is. And my mother, Esther Kamholz, who gave me this career advice as I left for my first job after college: "Choose your career carefully. You may be doing it the rest of your life!" Well Mom, I've done many things since then but choosing carefully has always been good guidance. I also want to thank my brother, Barry Katz, for invaluable tips about selling yourself and for sharing his experiences.

As for my wonderful in-laws, Angelo and Rosemarie Rigano, who shared insights and were role models in so many ways about how to conduct yourself at work and in life, I cannot thank them enough for years of believing that their daughter did not marry badly.

And finally, to the one person who believed first and most, my wife, Rita. Without her support, encouragement and help, whether in editing, listening, or simply keeping me on track, you would not be holding this book in your hands today. Many times I came home at night after a Job Support Meeting and went to the computer to write about what had transpired, and she never complained. For years of spending Wednesday nights alone while I ran the meetings and then putting up with me when I wrote and even more importantly when I felt I couldn't, I am forever and always in her debt.

TABLE OF CONTENTS

INTRODUCTION

The way people find jobs has changed. But one thing has not. Someone gets hired.

There are, on average, six people for every opening. Finding the opportunities and then getting the job has become more competitive than ever, and that's not expected to change in the foreseeable future.

At the end of 2008 and continuing in 2009, more than half a million people lost their jobs every month—more than 8 million jobs lost in one devastating year. Job losses of this magnitude are unprecedented in our working lifetimes. And most of the people who lost their jobs were completely unprepared for how to cope with the emotional and economic upheaval that followed.

Jobs were lost in every strata of the workforce. Senior executives who had steadily built their careers over the span of decades. Entry-level staff that were caught in the vise of "Last In, First Out." Low performers who were downsized but perhaps should have been managed out years ago. Solid citizens who came to work every day, did their jobs and never imagined that they'd be asked to leave before they chose to. Perhaps you recognize one of these people. Perhaps you are one of these people. As they carried their boxes of personal belongings to the parking lot as they left their buildings for the last time, they all had common thoughts.

"Why me?"

"How did it come to this?"

"Why didn't I see this coming?"

And the most frequent and most chilling, "What do I do now?"

This is a book that will help you begin to understand what's happened to you and provide a roadmap that helps you find your way through the multitude of doubts, fears and questions running through your head.

This is not a book of answers. It is a book of questions. Today, more than ever, to find the right answers, you have to be sure that you are asking the right questions. Questions about what you can do next. Questions about changing careers. About starting your own business. About creating your next opportunity. Is it the right time to do any of these things, based on the economy and your personal situation, and which are the best ones to consider? Which careers or industries are the ones most likely to flourish in today's global economy, and which are the ones for which your particular set of skills are best suited?

In 2009 most "experts" pointed jobseekers toward energy, education or healthcare. These are the fields that are supposedly recession-proof because there is a growing demand for expertise in all three and a growing demand for services in all three. But if none of these interests you, then what do you do? Or what if you are interested but have no experience in any of these fields? How do you make the transition? How do you convince the hiring manager that although you haven't worked in the field, you have the transferable skills that make you a viable candidate? And how do you do this in the first two minutes of a phone interview, when all you have to make your case is your voice, your enthusiasm and their 20-second review of your resume?

Some people are surprisingly confident when they lose their jobs. These people think they know exactly what to do and are shocked when timeworn techniques fail miserably. For those who think they have all the answers, this book is a chance to have your answers questioned. To think through and explore your strategies before you implement them. No matter how long it's been since you were last in the job market, it has changed. What worked before, even a year ago, is not likely to work the same way now. There are certainly many practices that remain consistently effective in today's environment. For decades people have said, "It's not what you know, it's who you know." That's still true. Only today we say, "Network, network, network." But how do you network? And with whom? This is a new skill that must be mastered to succeed in the job market or on the job today. Networking used to be face-to-face, or at the very least over the phone. Now it's Facebook or LinkedIn or Twitter. But beware of limiting your networking to the Internet. Truly effective networking still involves shoe leather and handshakes. You must create a strategy for turning your online connections into genuine network contacts. Your online connections may send some leads your way, but networks that lead to referrals and jobs must be cultivated and almost always involve a face-to-face meeting. In today's precarious environment, some people are tentative about recommending someone else for a position. Yes, we all understand the theory of good karma. If I help you, then when you've landed a job you will help me. Sure. But many people are hesitant to refer someone based solely on an online association because it's their own reputation that's at stake. Recruiters are known to prefer warm referrals to cold calls for the simple reason that people don't refer junk. People are afraid to risk their relationship with recruiters by referring someone who reflects poorly on them. For this simple reason, as comfortable as you may be in cyberspace, you need to meet with people in your network, as well as recruiters, in the flesh. This is the kind of networking that many people will go to great lengths to avoid. Yet it is this level of networking that yields the greatest rewards.

Twenty-five years ago, when I was a line manager and needed staff, all I did was let my current staff know that I was looking for people. Within days I had at least a half dozen qualified applicants and after a few interviews, settled on one. Later, while working in human resources at one of the largest banks in the country, I learned a number of more strategic and effective sourcing, screening and interviewing techniques. For the past ten years, as a consultant, trainer and career coach, I've worked with people on both sides of the hiring desk. It is this unique two-way perspective that makes this book invaluable.

This book will help you discover what you need to say and do to convince the interviewer, recruiter or hiring manager that you are the one. I will share my experience as a staffing professional and the insights I've gained through years of working with people who are interviewing to help you understand what's going on in the interviewer's head as she asks her questions and listens to your responses. In addition, I'll explain how to read her non-verbal signals so that you know when to continue and when the interview is over.

In 2002 I created and have since facilitated a weekly support group for people who are in transition. Originally it started out as a group for people who were unemployed. Fortunately, in a little over a year almost all of the original members of the group had either found jobs or other directions in life. Two went into business for themselves, others found new careers to pursue and still others found jobs in their professions.

Word of the success of the group spread. Suddenly I was hearing not only from people who were out of work but also from employed people who were concerned over the stability and security of their jobs. Others joined the group because they were bored, stifled, unfulfilled or worried that they had made a wrong choice somewhere along the line. The nature of the group changed.

The Job Support Group (JSG), as it is known, has become a place where people deal with the stress of losing a job, finding a job or keeping a job. It's a place where people at all levels and ages have come together to support each other and work through the seemingly interminable dilemma of finding their next job, career or passion.

Many of the stories in this book are gleaned from the experiences of these people as they tried to figure out what to do next and how to reinvent themselves. Many more come from the people with whom I have worked in my private practice and some come from my experience as a human resource professional for more than twenty years.

The truth is no one can figure out what you have to do to find a job except you. You may want a book that will tell you exactly what to do, but no book can. Not this book nor any other. What

14

this book will do is help you to pave the path to your next job. It will help you figure out what you might do, what you might want to do and what you can do. There are three spheres to consider. There's what you like to do; what you're good at; and what will allow you to make enough while doing it to meet your economic needs. The intersection of these three spheres is the sweet spot we all seek. Figuring out which is the dominant driver or motivator in your present circumstance is another part of the equation. Understanding that your drivers are not static but constantly shifting based on the economy, your needs and your wants further muddy the decision-making process.

This is a book for people who are employed, unemployed, underemployed and undecided.

Someone's gonna get hired. It might as well be you.

Let's get started.

One

THE JOB SEARCH ROLLER COASTER

Fasten your seatbelts!

When you lose a job, you're about to embark on a roller coaster of emotions. Some people like roller coasters. Some people (like me) hate them. But losing a job is a ride that no one looks forward to.

Think about roller coasters. There's that slow climb to the first peak and then a dizzying descent coupled with a rush of emotions. Then anticipation, panic, fear and exhilaration as you swoop down and around and then up again until you glide to a smooth landing. The job loss ride is somewhat different. Very often you never even see it coming. You're called to a meeting and the next thing you know, they've clamped the safety bar in front of you and you're off. But there is no slow anticipatory ascent as you prepare for the flood of emotions to come. Instead you're pushed off a cliff, starting with the speeding, breakneck tumble to the bottom before you can climb back up to that sought-after smooth landing. There are tunnels where you're plunged into darkness and can't even begin to imagine that you'll be able to find your way out. As you go through this bewildering experience, there are as many as ten emotional phases you can anticipate, ranging from loss and shame at the outset to the confidence and fulfillment you feel as you secure your next position.

The more you understand about the journey you've embarked on, the better you'll be able to survive the trip.

At the start of the roller coaster ride, you have a job. You're okay. Suddenly you are **unemployed**. You may then go through something like this:

- **Shame**, feeling that you have failed or done something wrong.
- **Anger** at whoever did this to you.
- A renewed sense of **loss** before you start to…
- Go through a **transition** which leads to…
- **Reinvention** of your self or your career.
- The **challenge** of turning your plan into reality.
- The **structure** you develop with your renewed sense of purpose.
- **Happiness** once you start to realize that this is working.
- **Confidence** that you will find employment.
- **Fulfillment** in the knowledge that you are once again in control of your career.

The more you understand each of these ten phases, the more adept you're going to be when dealing with the loss of a job. There you are, going to work every day, thinking you're safe and then, wham!

You've lost your job. You're unemployed. The first thing to recognize is that this is a loss. You can expect to feel all the pain associated with the loss of a loved one, even if you didn't love your job. Many people are surprised at how much they miss their old job. It's not necessarily because they loved it either. You, in fact, may have hated your job and dreaded having to show up every day. But it was your job. And you haven't just lost your job; you've lost your identity.

SO, WHAT DO YOU DO?

Think about the last time you met someone new, at a party, at a conference, at any kind of social gathering. What's one of the first things they ask you? "What do you do?" They're not talking about what you do in your spare time. They're not inquiring about your hobbies. They want to know what you do for a living. This is so they can figure out who you are based on their impressions of other people they know in the same profession. How do you feel when you have to answer that you are unemployed? You may want to say, "I'm an insurance underwriter." But then they may ask, "Who for?" Now you're caught. Do you lie? Do you mention the name of the firm that you used to work for? Do you claim to be a freelancer? In that job? Not likely.

For some, even scarier than the loss of income is the loss of identity. Many of us have heard the expression, "Your work is your worth." Although the statement isn't true, for many people work gives a foundation upon which to build the rest of our identities.

Think of it this way. If you asked an accountant what she does, the response might be, "I'm an accountant, a CPA. I take tests to certify my expertise and once I have that designation I can proclaim to the world that I am a smart and valuable person. I work pretty much between the hours of 8:30 and 5:30 except from January to early May, when I rarely see my family and expect to work a lot of weekends. I am a respected professional whose knowledge and opinions are sought out by many people trying to plan their financial future. This is a very important job I do. There is a clear progression in my field. If I choose, I may go into financial planning someday, or strive to make partner in a large firm. I can also pursue consulting as an option. When I meet new people and they find out that I am an accountant, they frequently hit me up for some free financial and even investment advice. While I find this a little annoying, I secretly revel in the opportunity to dish out my opinions. I like being respected for my ideas. I'm good with numbers and always wind up divvying up the check when out with friends because I can do this faster than everyone else. And no one questions what I tell them. I have a reputation for ethical behavior and discretion. I know things about people that they don't tell their spouses. I'm an accountant."

How much of that statement has to do with the actual work an accountant does and how much is self-perception? For many of us, work infiltrates our thinking and self-image. When that is wrenched away, you worry that others may question your skills, knowledge, ability and expertise. Then you may start to question yourself. This is when job loss becomes so much more than simply a loss of income. It becomes a loss of self. When you hurtle down the steep slope from having a job to losing a job, you may experience that emotional free fall that soon becomes shame.

HOW CAN I SHOW MY FACE IN PUBLIC?

Shame: The next twist on the roller coaster of emotions you may go through. I know people who, on the day they lost their job, didn't go home until after 5 p.m. to avoid having to tell their loved ones for as long as possible. They keep the mask on as long as they can, figuring that if they keep the facade in place maybe it didn't really happen. In the movie *The Full Monty* the character Gerald doesn't tell his free-spending wife for six months. He gets up each morning, gets dressed and goes off to "work" (actually to an employment center for laid-off workers) to keep up the appearance of having a job. It is only when the repo men show up and start carting appliances out of their home that his wife finds out. We'd like to think that would happen only in a movie. But I know people who have waited days to tell their family what has happened.

If the sense of loss is keen, the sense of shame can be paralyzing. Many people, especially the first time they lose a job, have no idea of how to handle it. Losing a job is what happens to other people. You think of all the unkind things you've thought or heard when people got fired or laid off. "Good riddance. What took management so long? He was never really that good. His department has been carrying him for a long time. He was an anchor, and it's about time they dropped him." You wonder, "Is that what's being said about me?"

The games your mind plays on you as you deal with the shame can be terrifying. This is why shame can be so paralyzing. You question your talents, your abilities and yourself. "Maybe I wasn't ever really that good? How did I wind up in this job anyway? I never wanted to be a database administrator." Even in a downsizing situation in which your abilities very often have very little to do with the decision to lay you off, you take it very personally. For the company, it's a business decision. For you, it's personal. You wonder, as you lie awake, "If only I had worked harder. If only I had done my job a little better. If only I had put in more overtime. If only I had spoken up at that meeting that my boss's boss attended. If only I had volunteered for that special project." If, if, if.

Shame can lead to depression. You turn inward. You don't want to see anyone; you don't want to talk to anyone. Especially not people with jobs! How could they understand what you're going through? And yet this is exactly what everyone is telling you to do. "Get out there. Network. Read the blogs, join chats, go on interviews, meet people." But that is the last thing you want to do in this phase. And possibly the last thing you should do.

I'm not recommending that you wallow in grief for an eternity, but look at yourself in this condition. Are you in the best frame of mind to present yourself in a positive light to an employer? Many people jump onto the interview carousel as soon as they are laid off. Get busy, get out there, get a job. Some people are able to do this, but they are rare. Yet these are the people you hear about. "Stephanie got laid off on Tuesday and she had a new job by Friday! More money and a shorter commute too!" You hate Stephanie. Relax. Stephanie is an urban legend who is as likely to exist as alligators in the sewers. For most people this is the worst time to look for a job. You're going to waste precious networking opportunities if, when you meet someone, you come across as a scared, anxiety-ridden victim with little confidence in your skills and no ability to put together a coherent sentence. Your resume, which you haven't kept up to date, is a mess. Two-and-a-half pages long and you forgot to include that big project you successfully coordinated two years ago. You haven't had to create a resume in more than ten years. How much should you include? Bullets or narrative? Chronological or functional? Should you have an objective or is that old fashioned? The thought of revising your resume can seem so nerve-wracking that it's easier to procrastinate, watch another episode of *Oprah* and wait for that perfect job to appear on Monster.

You need to heal. You need to allow yourself a little time to get over the loss and get past the shame. Grieving takes time. The longer you've been working, particularly if you've been working in one position or with one company, the harder it is to get over the loss and the longer it will take. How long? That's different for everyone. But you do need to decompress. You need to learn how to stop saying "we" when you refer to the company and start saying "they." I know one person who was with a company for almost twenty years when he was laid off. He was thinking of giving himself a day, maybe a week. I told him, to his shock and dismay, that these early phases might take as long as six weeks.

The good news is there are things that you can do during this period to help you get to where you want to be. Now is the time to start working on the resume. Catch up on your reading, both business and leisure. Start networking, but only so far as letting people know about your availability. Maybe you'll set up one or two meetings with people with whom you feel particularly comfortable, but stay inside your "first circle" of closest contacts (more on the circles later). Take walks. Clear your head. It's important to take care of yourself, both physically and emotionally because the next phase is sneaking up on you. It will show up when you least expect it with a ferocity that will surprise you.

"I'M MAD AS HELL AND I'M NOT GONNA TAKE IT!"

Anger. Shame becomes anger.

"How dare they do this to me?"

"I'll make them sorry they ever let me go!"

"I'll get even with them."

"They'll go straight into the crapper without me."

"Someday I'll own that company."

When you were ashamed, you blamed yourself. You thought that you'd done something wrong to bring this on yourself. Now you blame them. They did something wrong. To you! They did something to you! And when someone does something bad to you, you want revenge. And not only did they do something bad to you, they did it to your family! How dare they put your loved ones through this? Now you're getting really mad!

The anger phase can be white hot. You've gone from a dull ache to a searing pain. Before, you couldn't get to sleep. Now, you can't stay asleep. You wake up in the middle of the night sweating from such vivid dreams you're amazed to find that you're actually in your own bed. Your heart is pounding. The night is still, you're anything but. You calm down, but you can't get back to sleep. This only makes you angrier. They robbed you of your job, now they're robbing you of your sleep. The rest you need so you can find another job. Again you think, "How dare they?" You are the victim, the persecuted one.

Fortunately the anger phase can be brief—if you take control of the anger instead of letting the anger control you. Think about it. How many angry people have you hired? If someone came into your office for an interview and you sensed anger, hostility or mistrust of all employers, would you recommend that person for hire? So while for some the anger can actually become enjoyable (hey, who doesn't like bad-mouthing the people or companies they hate?) this is no place to settle down long term. You're not doing yourself, your job prospects or your career any favors by staying angry.

You must find a way to channel that anger into a more positive energy. Anger is exhausting. You're going to find that out pretty quickly. After you've spent a phone call, or a meeting, or an hour venting about what they did to you, you're going to want to sit down. Maybe take a nap. Maybe eat something you shouldn't. But none of these things gets you closer to your immediate goal, which is getting out of the anger phase and on with your job search.

The truth is, the facts probably lie somewhere between anger and shame. You didn't do anything wrong that made you lose your job, and they didn't do anything to you out of malice. Your employment was terminated, not you. You still exist, with all the talent, skills and ambition you had before. But now your ideas about who you are and what you want to do have been reshaped on the anvil of job loss. One of the things that white-hot anger can do is change your perspective on work, on your career, and on your future choices. Having experienced job loss once, you'll approach your next opportunity using a different lens to examine the position. Once you get past the anger, you'll be able to more clearly factor in the stability of the company, their history of hiring and layoffs, and the tenure of your new boss when you consider an opportunity. Is the work seasonal? Is this a growing or dying industry? Is this an industry that is prone to mergers, takeovers and acquisitions, all things that can lead to being downsized again through no fault of your own?

When the anger no longer clouds your thinking, you can figure out what to do next or where to look. You are starting on the path toward transition. There are lots of different ways to speed up the move past anger to the transition phase, but the first is to recognize that it will happen. You will get over this. You will eventually tire of being so angry all the time. You'll grow tired of lashing out at your loved ones, your friends, even strangers at the supermarket. You'll grow tired of looking for people to unload on. You may start to dislike the angry person you've become. That's good, because that's not you. Think back to the person you were back when you had a job. Sure, you were tired and overworked and sometimes cranky. But you were also productive, creative and contributing.

People take different paths to get away from the anger. Some exercise, some do yoga, some turn to their religion. You need to figure out what will work for you. I know someone who used this time to do volunteer work. His goal was to get past the anger and stop feeling sorry for himself by spending time with those who had even less than he did. Volunteering with the homeless, at a soup kitchen, for the local animal shelter or helping kids learn to read at a library are all ways to begin to feel more like a contributing member of your community. These are things you can do to get into a better frame of mind so that you can get on with and get back to your work life.

But watch out! There's a pothole ahead that you didn't even see. The next phase: it's **Loss** again. Some people look back to loss on their way from anger to the transition phase. But this time it's a different feeling of loss than before. This time you miss the self-righteous anger. You miss all the energy and heat you had when you were angry. This may sound strange. How can you miss being that angry, misanthropic being that lashed out at everyone around you? Because it gave you definition. You were The Victim. You were the injured party. You were the person who had a story to tell. And you got really good at telling it, maybe even embellishing it as you went along.

What's really happening is you're letting go again. It's not uncommon for people to feel that sense of loss again, because letting go of the anger means really letting go of the old job once and for all. Of course you're not really letting go of the old you, just your old work identity. At this point you're admitting that who you were and how you once defined yourself is truly gone, and now you are about to embark on the very difficult job of reinventing yourself. This is where the loss comes in again. You're no longer an IBM'er or a Citi-banker or a Prudential agent. You're just you, and you're not sure who you're about to become. Pretty scary, but pretty exciting too.

This loss phase will be shorter than the first one. You've already been through it, so you'll recognize it for what it is. You won't be as paralyzed. The sense of blame, of having done something wrong, will be tempered by the knowledge that it was a combination of factors – some of your doing, some decided by your former employer and some just based on the economy—that conspired to put you in the position you're in. The emotional hole you may find yourself in won't be as deep. The immediate goal is nearer and clearer too. There's a more apparent path away from the anger and the loss. You're getting closer to the transition phase.

The next two phases in your journey are transition and reinvention. Transition is the next step toward reinvention. Recognize that these are two separate phases. Many people want to skip or rush through transition, but as any woman who has ever given birth can tell you, you aren't going to give birth to a new person without getting through transition. Transition is a separate part of childbirth from delivery. Transition is a lot of hard work that you need to do before you get to the payoff of discovering that new person. This, for some people, is one of the most difficult and even painful parts of the process.

WHAT DO YOU WANT TO BE WHEN...?

Transition means getting ready. Transition means doing a lot of soul searching about what you want to be when you reinvent yourself next. We are constantly reinventing ourselves. Whenever you learn a new skill, take on a new project or accept a new challenge, you reinvent yourself. Every time you endeavor to do something that you have never done before, a new you appears. Only this time you feel like there's a lot more riding on your decisions. This time you feel that there is no safety net. The decisions you make now about what you are going to do and who you are going to become are for real. You are no longer playing with house money. Before, if you tried something new and failed, you still had your job. Now, there's a whole lot more riding on your decisions.

Transition also means looking into yourself and thinking long and hard about what you've been doing for the past five or ten years, or longer. "How did I ever wind up as a Customer Service

Manager? I don't even like people!" But somehow that's what you became. Maybe because someone told you that you were good at it. Maybe because it just seemed like the natural progression from that first job you got as a customer service representative. That job was easy to get and easy to keep. You thought that you'd only do it for a couple of years while you figured out what you really want to do. But then they made you a team leader. They rewarded you for doing a good job and after a few more years they made you a supervisor, and the next thing you knew, ten years had passed and you were fighting for that Customer Service Manager job. Once you got the job it meant more hours and more headaches, but you had reached a position of respect and responsibility. Then the customer service function was outsourced to another part of the country (or the world) where the labor was cheaper (I wish I was making this up, but you know I'm not) and you find yourself on the roller coaster.

So now you're forced to deal with the responsibility of finding another job. But you're also faced with the opportunity to figure out the best road to choose. Transition means taking stock of all your skills and talents and figuring out where they can be best used. It's the chance to explore the intersection of what you like to do and what you're good at doing. Transition means taking a very objective assessment of yourself and figuring out what to do next and who to try to become. There are many steps to this process that will be discussed in greater depth in later chapters of this book, but for now suffice to say that transition entails doing an honest reality check of who you are and who you want to become. Then you'll have to reposition yourself so that future employers can look at your particular mix of skills and abilities and see how you will fit into their organizations in a mutually beneficial way.

Another part of the transition phase is to figure out how your particular skills and experiences best position you to succeed in the current economy and job market. The potential economic impact of the choices you make are one reason this phase can be so difficult or painful, which is why many people retreat back to what they've always done instead of taking the opportunity to move ahead to reinvention. This part is scary. I have worked with people who understand and agree with and recognize every phase up to this point. But now they are looking into the abyss. "Do I really want to make a major change? Am I ready to redefine who I am after all these years? Will my friends, my family, my network take me seriously or laugh at me?" Fear, shame, anger—they have all led you to this point. Retreating back down the hill is not an option, because you are near the bottom of the roller coaster ride. You can try to go back to what you've always been or you can climb up to where you want and dream to be. You're going to be making very difficult decisions about yourself, your future and the world of work out there.

Some people will shy away because they feel that they are not good at making life decisions. "I was never very good at forecasting the future. I didn't get involved in strategic decisions at work because I was always a more reactive, tactical person. The market scares me, that's why I've always invested in mutual funds instead of individual stocks. I don't know where to start. I'll go back and look for a job in my old profession." These are the excuses people make. To themselves and to others. You can make a very good case for why going back to your old kind of job is the best move to make. "It's safe. It will protect my family. I know that I can do it. It will be easier to convince people who can hire me to hire me because they'll know what I can do and I'll be able to convince them that I can do it." And sometimes looking in your current field is the right choice.

But in many cases your old job went to India. Or Costa Rica or Ireland. The choice to go back to your old job may be a dead end, or at best, postponing the inevitable. You may be putting off the decision to reinvent yourself now because it seems too risky, but it's not going to be any less risky in a couple more years. And here's one more reason to do it now (as if you need one): a couple of years from now you'll be a couple of years older. Unfortunately, that means it will be even harder to make the transition to a new job, a new industry or a new career.

So what are you waiting for? Are you waiting to have the "I'm too old" excuse? A woman wanted to go back to college once all her children had completed their college educations. While talking to a friend, and trying to talk herself out of doing it, she concluded with this thought. "I'm fifty-eight years old. It'll take me four years to finish my degree. In four years I'll be sixty-two!"

Her friend replied calmly, "If you don't go back to school, how old will you be in four years?"

Reinvention. Finally, the phase you thought you'd start doing as soon as you lost or left your last job. Didn't think it'd take this long to get here, did you? But after all the angst, anger, pain, shame and introspection, you've reached a point in your development where you can start to look for the answer to the question "What will I be when I reinvent myself next?"

That's really the question to ask. In countless exchanges and discussions with people who are exploring their options, I ask them to finish this sentence.

"What do you want to be when you…?"

"Grow up" is how they invariably and immediately chime in.

But the answer is "reinvent yourself next." Next because you may do this more than once. Next because reinvention is a process, not a destination. Next because the more control you take over your destiny, the more planning you do for your future, the more you craft your career, the less vulnerable you are to the whims and vagaries of the economy and the market.

Besides, you are grown-up already. Going through the process of reinvention, trying to figure out what you're going to do with the next two or five or ten years of your life is a very grown-up thing to do. When people respond with "When I grow up," it's usually accompanied by a sheepish grin or a shrug of the shoulders. People are embarrassed by having to start over. Why? There is nothing to be ashamed of in figuring out what it is you want to do next at any stage of your life. There's no need for that feeling of failure or shame to be seeping in again. Whether you lost your last job or you're working to figure out what your next career step will be, this is a time for celebration and exuberance. You're not going to explore your options thoroughly unless you are fully committed to the idea of making this change. If you lost your job, very often it's not because you did anything wrong. So don't be embarrassed or ashamed of searching for something more fulfilling.

Sometimes people will disparage you for taking the time to consider your options so carefully.

"What do you mean you're exploring your options? You're a social worker. Just look for another social work job! Don't you think it's a little irresponsible to waste all this time 'exploring your options'? You're not a kid, you know. Just go get a job."

These people may be threatened by the idea of reinvention. They've never had to do it or never chose to do it. Not everybody is ready or able to take on the heavy lifting of career transition and reinvention. So people who feel threatened by your taking the time to do it sometimes try to discourage you. Don't let them. What you're doing is wonderful, though you might not always think so as you're going through it. You're taking steps to ensure that your reinvention will go more smoothly. Once you've gotten into the habit of planning for your future success, you're not likely to be thrown by change when it is thrust upon you.

The process of reinvention is exhilarating. You're starting on the upside of the roller coaster now. It means you have a lot of climbing to do and you may not always see where the next ledge is. You may want to rest a while, but at the same time you want to see what's over the next crest. Once you figure out what it is that you're working toward, you want to keep moving. It's like Billy Crystal's character says near the end of the movie *When Harry Met Sally*. "When you realize you want to spend the rest of your life with someone, you want the rest of your life to start as soon as possible." When you figure out what it is that you want to be doing next, you'll want to start doing it as soon as possible.

CLIMBING OUT OF THE HOLE

Having figured out how you're going to reinvent yourself, you now face the **Challenge**. It is a challenge to turn your plan into reality. You may think that the hard part is done and now you just go on to the new you. It's not that simple. The phases will come quickly now as you figure out the challenges you face in implementing your plan. This is another time when people get discouraged. You think you've figured it all out, but all you've figured out is what you're going to do next, not how you're going to get there. It might mean going back to school. If you're in a job, it might mean making a lateral move to get where you want to go. It might mean making sacrifices as you take a pay cut to get started in your new chosen field. Don't get discouraged. You've come so far that it will be just as painful to go back as it will to keep going forward. And you're so close to the most rewarding phases that going forward is the only realistic option.

The next thing you have to do, once you've identified the challenge, is to define the **Structure**. You're going to figure out a plan of action, the steps you need to take to get to where you've decided you want to be. For some people this is the fun part. They love planning, figuring out every action to take, the logical progression, the whys and wherefores. But some people hate it. They're more spontaneous. "I'm not a planner, I'm a doer. I'll just jump in and see how it works out. If I make a mistake, I'll just start over." While that optimism is to be applauded, you'll get where you want to be a lot faster with a little careful planning. If you're the type of person who enjoys and luxuriates in the planning phase, go to town. Your time is now. This is when you start to rediscover some of your strengths. The same planning skills that made you successful on the job are now going to make you successful as you look for a job. If planning is not where you see your strengths, this phase will be more of a challenge but it is one you must go through nonetheless. You know what they say about failing to plan.

Once you have a structure, you'll be able to follow each of the steps as you climb out of the depths into which you've descended. You'll know what to do, where to go, whom to contact. You'll start to gain some traction and accelerate. You're on your way.

YOU ARE ABOUT TO BE SURPRISED

You haven't gotten to where you want to be yet, you haven't gotten that new or next job, but one day you will be amazed to find that you're experiencing **Happiness**. Yes, happiness. Because you'll start to find that you're getting some positive feedback about your journey. Even before you get that new job, you're exhibiting some positive vibes, some excitement about what you're doing. You are reinventing yourself. You're moving with purpose and direction. You know what you're going to achieve, what you're going to become. You start behaving like a person who knows what she's doing. You have a reason to get up in the morning and things to accomplish. If you're currently employed in a job that's sapping the life out of you and are reinventing yourself while working, suddenly the job you're in doesn't bother you as much. You realize you're not going to be doing it forever. During the happiness phase you'll have a spring in your step, a smile on your face and your favorite song on your iPod. You're happy with who you are and where you're going.

This happiness will result in **Confidence**, the next phase, and generally where you'll see the results of all the hard work you've being doing. When you are confident, people want to be around you. Those people in your network who you were afraid would shun you are happy to take your calls because you are brimming with excitement. You are on the brink of something wonderful, something inspiring.

This is the time to book those interviews. This is the time to get out there. When you have the confidence in your ability and in your decisions, there's nobody who can stop you. You will run into people who will question your choice but you have the answers. When they say, "Do you really think you can cut it in finance? You were never that good with numbers," you're ready. "Of course I can. I've got the skills, I've improved my knowledge and expertise with Excel and numbers don't challenge me the way they used to." You are so confident you can easily acknowledge their doubts, expressed as concern: "You're right. I used to not be so good with numbers and I was always afraid, but now I know how to use the software to check my work and I can make my spreadsheets jump up and do the Macarena. Numbers are no longer a challenge for me, but thanks for your concern." That's confidence.

You will be amazed at how good you feel at this part of the ride. You are so close to completion that the landing will be almost anti-climactic. This isn't to say that you'll be offered the first job you go for, although this has happened with some people with whom I've worked. The speed with which they got a job caught them by surprise. They were all set for the long haul and boom; their job search was over. You've reached the next phase.

IT'S A WONDERFUL LIFE

Fulfillment. This is not a destination. You've reached the next phase and it's where you hopefully will be spending a lot of time. It might be a new job. It might be a promotion. It might be a new career in a wholly different function. It might be doing the same job but for a different organization, one that provides the fulfillment you seek in other ways. It's closer to home and your commute is shorter. It makes a product you can believe in. Overtime is rare and you can actually get home to have dinner with your family.

However you define fulfillment, this is what you've been working toward. Many people get fulfillment from their jobs, others from the flexibility that their jobs afford them. Some from the financial freedom the position allows. You'll know when you get here because you will have defined fulfillment long ago in the transition and reinvention phases.

Fulfillment means different things to different people. Later on we'll discuss how fulfillment may come from your job or new career or it may come from having the time to do other things. It's usually not measured in dollars and cents. Many people seek financial security. A few seek real financial wealth. Different things motivate people but I have found that people who are solely motivated by their paycheck rarely find fulfillment. It has been said that the person who is content with what they have is the richest person of all. Think of George Bailey at the end of *It's a Wonderful Life*. Rich? No. Fulfilled? Well, if you have to ask, then it's time for you to rent that movie again.

You've come to the end of your roller coaster ride. There have been a few bumps, a few unexpected plunges and some groping in the dark. But now you've found that Promised Land where the work is challenging, the rewards are appropriate and the overtime is manageable. However you define fulfillment, you're ready to move ahead in your new job or new field armed with the knowledge that you know how to navigate one of the scariest and most unpredictable rides around. You can confidently move ahead to your next challenge without the nagging fear of losing your job because you have developed the skills to cope with and thrive through one of the most challenging events that can happen.

Two

WHEN WILL I GET LAID OFF?

And what can I do to prevent it?

Downsized. RIF'd. Externally reallocated. Employment status adjustment. At liberty. Whatever you call it, it's not good. Thousands of people, good people, lose their jobs every month. They didn't underperform at their job. They didn't steal anything or start a fight in the cafeteria.

The company simply made a decision to:

"go in another direction,"

"explore its options,"

"reprioritize its initiatives" or

"reassess its positioning in the market."

And people just like you got caught in the squeeze.

These are not terminations for cause. Since the late '70s and accelerating through the '80s and '90s companies looking for a way to cut expenses go for the low-hanging fruit. That's why so many employees today feel like they are walking around with a bull's-eye on their back.

WHEN SHOULD I WORRY?

There is a cycle to layoffs. You can almost predict them. In some industries they are as regular as the swallows returning to Capistrano. The first thing you need to understand is that from the time a large or midsize organization decides that downsizing is the way to go, it usually takes four to six weeks before anyone is let go. Even if the company is simply going to swing the axe and lop 10% from every department, these things take time. To properly assess the people and prepare all the exit paperwork and work out the schedule of when to do it and who's going to say what to whom and how to make sure that HR has checked and double checked everything for adverse impact, it's simply going to take a long time. It can take even longer if the organization is going to make more judicious cuts to actually make the reductions in force ("RIFs") a strategic, rather than a panic, decision.

Think about the annual cycle that businesses go through. In January, most organizations are focusing on closing the books on the previous year, taxes, and creating the new strategic plan for the coming year. They meant to have the strategic plan completed before year-end, but it didn't get done. So now the senior team is looking at how it will get things done this year. If the decision is made that there's too much fat and something needs to be done, then as sure as there are golden parachutes for the senior executives, someone's going to go. But once that decision is made sometime in mid-to-late January, it's going to take some time to implement. So the first danger zone of the year is mid-February until the end of March. Perhaps the senior execs don't want to ruin their long holiday weekend feeling bad about the gold watch employee who got canned, so very often the layoffs don't hit until after President's Day weekend. But then, watch out. From President's Day until the end of March, bean counters of every variety are on the lookout for every cent they can save. And if the savings can be done in the first quarter, the organization will reap an even greater payoff.

So now it's April 1st and you still have a job. April Fools! You're still not safe. It's likely that cuts will slow down in April. Finance needs to assess the impact of the first quarter cuts. The executives who had to do all the actual talking to the released employees need a break. There's work to be done that got put off while everyone was wondering if they still had a job. This is another ugly truth about layoffs. On the one hand there is the fear factor that motivates employees to work even harder when the rumor of layoffs starts going around. Just so you know, this is a waste of your time. When the senior team is huddled with finance and HR trying to figure out who's going to be let go, they're not looking at what you're doing, they're looking at what you've done. So the overtime you're putting in will not save you. Others take the opposite approach and productivity drops because people figure, "What the hell, the decision's probably already been made, why bust my tail if they're going to fire me? If I'm still around I'll have to pick up the slack. I'll get back up to speed then." Most organizations see a drop in productivity in reverse proportion to the number of rumors flying around. And an uptick in paper usage as everyone starts printing copies of their resumes.

So April, with its Easter and Passover holidays, is usually a time for quiet reflection. But while you're reflecting, senior management is realizing, "We didn't cut deep enough! We thought this would do it, but we're still not going to make budget!" Back to the drawing board and once again managers are trying to figure out where the cuts will be made. Again, it takes about four to six weeks to pull together The List, and for HR to review it and determine that it will not result in too many lawsuits. It needs to be done before the end of the second quarter to get the maximum bang for the buck. Thus, the cuts need to be implemented well before July 4th. It's bad business to look unpatriotic. Cutting American jobs on or around Independence Day means the stock price will take a hit. So Danger Zone Number Two is May 15th until June 15th. If there were no first quarter cuts, this danger zone could start even earlier in May.

The lazy hazy crazy days of summer are indeed a time to catch your breath. Most companies do not have reductions during July, August, or September. Is it a sudden benevolence that has come over the U.S. corporate office? Not by a long shot. Too many people take vacation during these months. We can't be cutting heads when we already have too few people left to keep the place running. So for the most part, the summer is a quiet time for layoffs. But not to be nice to the workers. The senior staff who have to figure these things out and deliver the bad news want to take their vacation too. It takes a lot of time to plan and carry out a round of layoffs. There'll be time enough in the fall.

However, there are exceptions to this summer hiatus. Organizations that need to make cuts but fear the consumer backlash of cutting jobs often do the deed over the summer. The premise is that fewer people in the mainstream are paying attention to what Corporate America is doing during the summer. Who wants to read the Wall Street Journal when there's a new John Grisham novel? But beware September.

THE MOST PERILOUS TIME OF THE YEAR

No matter how old we get, we are all hardwired to the school calendar. September means back to school, and for those involved in layoff decisions it often means back to work. September is when forecasters start to look at end of year numbers. Are we going to make it? Will it be close? Do we need to tighten our belts, reduce expenses? You know what this means. One more round of cuts before the end of the year. But this time of year has its own set of parameters. If an organization starts looking at and thinking about cuts in September, the earliest that anyone will be notified will be right after the Columbus Day weekend. This is the time of year when there are more downsizings than any other, as more and more organizations try to meet the end-of-year profitability forecasts that were made back in January. Mid-October through mid-November is the third and final danger zone, and the most perilous. According to John Challenger, chief executive of the outplacement firm Challenger, Gray & Christmas, more people will be laid off in this small window of the year than any other.

It used to be that Columbus Day to Veteran's Day (how ironic considering the number of older workers whose jobs are eliminated) was the peak layoff season. The reason is primarily the calendar. Get this done before we get too close to Thanksgiving, Chanukah, Christmas and Kwanzaa. Get these people off the books before we have to pay out year-end bonuses. This is our last chance to make the year-end statements look good.

But this is one danger zone that has grown. Of late, some organizations have kept the layoffs going right up until Thanksgiving, and in a few instances, when all the paperwork could not be completed, even in the small window after Thanksgiving but before it got too close to Christmas. If you are still employed around December 15th, relax. Go to the office holiday party, raise a glass to those no longer with the company and share stories with your co-workers about how much more work there is to do now that there are so few people around to do it. Your jobs are safe. Until the next round starts. And it starts before the eggnog has curdled in your plastic cup.

It's important to recognize that not every organization is going to suffer through multiple RIFs throughout the year. I've seen companies in which it happened just as I described above. Usually an organization will go through one round of cuts a year if suffering a down year financially or restructuring their business. But remember that we are going through times like we've never seen before, and yours might be an organization that becomes a "serial downsizer." Senior management makes a slight reduction and then hopes for the best. But hope is not a strategy. It's not uncommon that an organization, trying to avoid appearing cruel and heartless, fails to make an adequate reduction. That's when the "employee headcount adjustments" go on and on and on...

IS THERE ANYTHING I CAN DO?

The silver lining to all this is that there are things you can do, strategies you can use to try to lessen the likelihood that you will be the one tapped on the shoulder and summoned to your manager's office. People have tried all kinds of different approaches to avoid the axe. Before you undertake any of these, you need to consider the likelihood for success. Which one you initiate depends on you, your feelings about the organization and your relationship with your manager.

The Mushroom

There's an old joke about employees being treated like mushrooms (they keep us in the dark and cover us with you-know-what), but when it comes to downsizings, you definitely don't want to be a mushroom. What's a mushroom in this environment? A mushroom is something that sticks its head up only to get cut off. So common wisdom is to keep your head down. Workers have practiced this approach for years yet it's not terribly effective. Lots of people think that if they just keep their nose to the grindstone, or nowadays the keyboard, no one will think of them. But these decisions are not made by some steely-eyed commandant patrolling the office floor peering out from behind a monocle. You are a name on an organization chart and if headcount is being reduced, one day they may get to you.

The 24/7

This is the person who seems to move into her office. As rumors swirl, she is always there. She shows up before anyone else and is the last to leave. This person has two theories for her behavior. The first is "I have made myself indispensable!" The second is "Look at the number of hours I'm working! I'm doing the work of two people!" Both of these strategies are flawed. Organizations today measure results, not hours. What's more, as more offices become virtual, the 24/7 approach is even less effective. No one even sees how much you're there. Your boss may be in Frankfort, Kentucky, or Frankfurt, Germany. Decisions are made based on your output. As for making yourself irreplaceable, next time you drive by a cemetery, think of all the irreplaceable people there. If you actually are doing the work of two people, how long can you reasonably keep this up? How long can you maintain the kind of quality needed to keep your boss satisfied? Eventually you will slow down, slack off or screw up. That's when they'll get you. Go home, take a shower and figure out how to produce the kind of results that will keep you in your job.

The Starchaser

This is the person who often risks a broken nose if the person above them on the organization chart stops short. You know what I mean. This is not the best way to insure that you will avoid the axe. First of all, you may pick the wrong star. I have seen many six-figure managers wind up on the wrong side of the exit interview desk. Second, this behavior has become more and more transparent. People in the office know what this person is doing and recognize the Starchaser for who he or she is—an opportunistic suck-up who has mastered the art of managing his manager and makes little, if any, other contribution to the organization. The fluidity in organizations today make this a less and less effective strategy, but don't be surprised if you see co-workers acting awfully strange when the boss is around.

The Dirty Worker

This strategy isn't as bad as it sounds. The Dirty Worker is not to be confused with the Backstabber (who needs no introduction). I certainly do not endorse the Backstabber's methods and tactics. But the Dirty Worker approach is an admirable option to stay employed. This is the person who takes on or accepts or even volunteers for the tasks no one else wants to or likes to do, yet must be done. In finance it might be an auditing position. In human resources it might be the person who takes on the job of rewriting Family and Medical Leave Act and Leave of Absence policies. Every organization needs "solid citizens," the "good soldiers" who are "in the trenches" and show up every day and do the essential functions that must be carried out. None of the glamour of sales or marketing. None of the heady responsibility of strategic planning. These are the drones, the worker bees, the common clay of the American workforce. Without them corporations can't exist. The key is to make sure, to the best of your ability, that you aren't doing a job that someone else thinks can be done more cheaply if outsourced. It needs to be a key function of onerous description. This job won't be fun, but it will be there.

The Volunteer

This unusual but sometimes successful approach is one I prefer and have used myself. When I say volunteer, I don't mean a volunteer to be laid off. That's the Handraiser ("Take me! Take me! Ooooooh, please take me!") The Handraiser is the person who wants to get a severance package as seed money to move on to his or her next venture, whether it is relocating or starting a business or early retirement. The Volunteer is the person who, at the first rumor of a merger or acquisition which is often the precursor to a round of layoffs, starts volunteering for every merger-related assignment he can. He tries to get on task forces, project teams, focus groups, whatever he can. This is a networking opportunity. It is highly likely that following a merger, an acquisition or a downsizing, you may find yourself working somewhere else in the organization. The people who are heading up these committees are the people who will be running the organization after the smoke clears. Take this opportunity to meet as many of these people as possible. This is not to make yourself indispensable, but is a way to insure that your name gets out there. It is also a way to re-introduce yourself to people you already know who may not have thought of you as anything but that guy in operations or the woman in payroll. Show them all what you have to offer to the new organization. Show them you are fearless. If you seem not to be afraid of losing your job, by making yourself even more visible, you are the "Anti-Mushroom." You may very well be the kind of person the organization realizes that it wants to keep.

USE A LITTLE TLC

What goes without saying is that the common denominator of any strategy to keep your job is TLC. Talent, luck and competency.

Talent is what got you your job in the first place. You must do your job well and you need the talent and skills to get the work done. But what got you here won't necessarily keep you here. You need to continually improve and refine your current skills as well as develop new ones. Talent was your ticket of admission, but talent alone won't keep you in your seat.

Luck will always play a factor in these outcomes. Corporations are constantly looking for other corporations to buy or to be acquired by. The marketplace is an elastic and fluid thing that does not stand still. There are certain things over which you have no control. Is your company the acquired or the acquirer? This is where luck comes in.

Competency is different from talent. Competency is the collection of behaviors you develop and the skills you enhance to get along with others and behave in a way that is consistent with the organizational norms of your company. Competencies are sometimes called the soft skills but I resist this term. Why do people call them "soft" when it's so hard to get them right? I prefer to call these strategic skills. These are the skills that transcend function. They are critical to success in any field. Once mastered, these can take you anywhere. In certain situations, these can even make up for gaps in your talent.

The final decision you need to make is: do you want to get laid off? Strange question, you may think, but you need to take into account many factors as you craft your career. Is it time to make a change? Do you want to be the last one out the door or gone in the first wave to hopefully bigger and better things? Are you feeling stale in your current function? Is relocation a possibility? Is yours a dying industry or does it have a robust future? What's the merger and acquisition landscape in your industry? Sometimes, if you've been through a restructuring before, you're in no mood to go through it again. In that case you may adopt the mentality of "do it to them before they do it to you." Many people dread losing their job, but for others, it couldn't have happened at a better time. You need to assess what's going on in your company, in your industry and in your life as you make this critical decision.

So the question these days is not if you will be laid off but when. Will that make it any less painful? No. But keep your head up and your wits about you and it is less likely to catch you by surprise. Properly anticipate what may happen to you, and when, and you will be better prepared. This will make the recovery time from this unpleasant event that much shorter. You'll be that much closer to your next career and your next reinvention.

Organizations keep coming up with incredibly inventive names to describe the act of separating you from your job. For your amusement and disbelief, below is a compilation of words and phrases to describe this all-too-frequent phenomenon. If you have heard other words or phrases and would like to share them, please do so at www.SGGH.net. Thanks.

Asked to Resign	External Reallocation	Prime-sizing
Career Assessment	of Resources	Reconfigured
and Re-Employment	Force Reduction	Redeployment
(CARE!)	Forced Career	Redirected
Career Transition	Transition	Redundancy
Chemistry Change	Given Liberty	Elimination
Coerced Transition	Indefinite Idling	Released
Decruited	Involuntary Separation	Reorganization
Dehiring	Job Separation	Requested Departure
Deployment	Made Available to the	Restructured
Deselected	Industry	RIF—Reduction in
Destaffing	Mutually Agreed Upon	Force
Discharged	Transition	Right-sizing
Dismissal	Negotiated Departure	Selected Out
Displacement	Offboarded	Selectively Separated
Downsizing	Off-ramped	Skill Mix Adjustment
Early Retirement	Outplaced	Terminated
Employment Status	Personnel Surplus	Transitioned
Adjustment	Reduction	Vocational Relocation
Excessed	Position Elimination	Workforce Imbalance
Exited	Position Redefinition	Adjustment

Three

HOW DO I LOOK
FOR A JOB?

When I haven't done it in 20 years!

One week at my Job Support Group, Patty said, "I just want to know what to do when I wake up in the morning so I can find a job. Is there a book out there that can tell me that?'"

I replied, "Yes. There are lots of books out there that will tell you exactly what they think you should do to find a job. And if they were thinking of you when they wrote that book, then their plan will work for you."

The truth is, no one can figure out what you have to do to find a job except you. You may want a book that will tell you exactly what to do, but no book will. Not this book or any other. What this book will do is help you to pave that path to your next job. It will help you figure out what you might do, what you might want to do and what you can do. This is a book for people who are employed, unemployed, underemployed and undecided.

SO, WHAT DON'T YOU WANT TO DO NOW?

Patty had worked at the same company for almost 13 years. Five years earlier a much larger, and distant, competitor had acquired the company. Over those five years there had been numerous restructurings that always resulted in people losing their jobs.

But Patty had always been retained. She was operating under the mistaken belief that it would never happen to her. Which is why it was such a shock when she got the notice that her employment was being terminated in the latest round of reductions. She hadn't looked for a job in over a decade. While her skills were still current and in demand, her situation was such that she could not afford a period of unemployment. Shortly after her initial visit to the JSG, she found a consulting assignment that paid well and interested her. Patty had never consulted or been a contract employee before, but she signed on. Although not a salaried, benefits-eligible position, the money was good and the assignment long-term, likely 18 to 24 months.

Five months later Patty was back at the JSG. The project had gone on hiatus. The salaried employees went onto other projects. Contract workers and consultants went out the door with virtually no notice. Now she didn't know what to do and was looking for a roadmap where no road existed.

She felt like she was back at square one (she wasn't), that she had wasted half a year (she hadn't) and she just wanted to pull the covers over her head and stay in bed (she couldn't). In fact she was well beyond square one because she had learned something very valuable, so the past five months were not a waste. And pulling up the covers, well, that just wasn't an option.

We probed to find out how Patty felt about the work she had done. She enjoyed the work and the people with whom she interacted, but she still felt very negative about the experience. Some of this came from the way the work ended, but more of the feelings came from the uncertainty and ambiguity of the whole situation. She never felt truly part of the team because she was an "outsider," never made to feel part of the organization, despite the vital contributions she was making.

Patty had been so wrapped up in the work that she hadn't taken the time to analyze how she felt while on the assignment. She also had allowed herself to daydream that her good work on this assignment might lead to an offer of full-time salaried employment, which in reality was not likely. This made the second release in six months that much harder to take and was one reason why she felt so lost.

"What did you learn from this experience?" I asked. She started to tell me the technical ins and outs of the project. "What did you learn about you?" I interrupted.

"I learned I don't want to be a consultant!" she blurted.

Exactly. Not everyone is cut out to move from project to project, from job to job. Some people are energized by this experience. These people could not imagine going to the same office, doing the same work for the same employer for 13 years. These people, if they lose a job, are not so overwhelmed by feelings of despondency or failure. It's just a signal that it's time to move on to the next assignment. The very important lesson that Patty had learned in these five months was that she was not cut out to be a consultant. She also learned that she did not want to be part of a smaller organization that utilized many consultants to fill in for positions that may or may not be around for long. In other words, Patty had learned that she wanted to work for a large corporation with extensive staff and much internal opportunity. Stability of the organization and having a routine were huge motivators in deciding for whom she wanted to work.

TARGETING YOUR SEARCH

One of the most important aspects of a job search is figuring out what you don't want. Patty had started to narrow the focus of her job search. Now it would be simpler to decide whether to send in that next resume and where to send it. She had begun a targeted search, one that has a much greater likelihood of success.

It has been reputed that Michelangelo was asked how he could find "The David" in a block of marble. He replied, so it is said, that he just chipped away everything that wasn't David.

This is also a strategy for figuring out what it is you want to do in your next job or next career.

Many people want the perfect job but don't know what they're looking for. They pore over the listings online or in the paper and can't figure out which posting to respond to. Or they apply to everything, using a scattershot "spaghetti on the wall" technique.

Sometimes it's easier to figure out what you don't want. Try looking through the listings and eliminate every job that you couldn't imagine or couldn't consider doing. Then go back and try to figure out why the job is so unappealing. Make a list of all the unappealing characteristics of these jobs, and then figure out what are the opposite, positive characteristics you want in your next job. You're now on the road to figuring out what you are looking for in a job.

Much of the frustration of the job search comes from the seemingly endless string of rejection. No one likes rejection. It hurts. It hacks at our self-esteem and makes it harder to get out of bed in the morning (or afternoon!) to tackle the incredibly difficult job of finding a job. One key to a successful search is to not waste time and energy on postings that are not likely to garner even an interview. If you keep spreading your resume blindly around the Internet, you're not really increasing the likelihood of finding a position; you're actually reducing it.

Some people respond to every posting that satisfies even a quarter of their requirements, if they have thought about what their requirements, other than salary, are at all. The belief is, "If I send out enough resumes one of them will land on the right desk." And it's so easy today. A few clicks and voila! This scattershot approach rarely results in a hit. This approach takes time away from the work of finding a good job, rather than just a job. Instead of a software engineer using the time to reply to every job with the initials "IT" in it, he is better served by taking the time to determine what defines a good job at this moment. What was a good job at 25 is rarely a desirable position in your 40s.

It's hard work to determine what makes a good job, which is why so many people opt for the scattershot approach. "I'm so busy! I must have sent out 50 resumes today" is a refrain I've often heard. I'd rather hear "I worked so hard today. I sent out only two resumes." That's the difference between a targeted search and an unfocused one. The philosopher Blaise Pascal once said, "I have made this [letter] longer, because I have not had the time to make it shorter." In that same vein, instead of doing the hard work of editing your choices to send a resume to one or two postings for which you are truly qualified and interested, it is easier to send out 50 and hope that through random chance and sheer volume you include the really good ones. Unfortunately, we often get so busy being busy that we forget what we are doing. Then we get exhausted, frustrated and dejected because nothing's coming through. But this is the result of our own inefficiency.

WHAT ARE PEOPLE SAYING ABOUT THIS COMPANY?

There are many other things you can do to better target an organization that is in sync with your work philosophy. Obvious things like checking their website but also searching the Internet for articles and write-ups of the organization. Their website is mostly propaganda in the sense that this is what they want people to know about their organization. Find out what other people are writing about the company. For every "www.CompanyName.com" site on the web, there may be a "www.CompanyNameSucks.com" as well. See what former employees (who have frequently created these sites) are saying while recognizing that these people are just as biased as the company website might be, only in the opposite direction. Check out other sites like www.jobvent.com or www.workrant.com. How prominently represented is the company you're considering on these sites? Search the websites of prominent business publications or the primary newspaper from the city in which the organization is headquartered. Very often the local newspaper will have things that don't find their way into the *Wall Street Journal*, the *New York Times* or *Forbes* magazine. If the organization is publicly traded, their annual report will be available in certain libraries or possibly online. Look at their competitor's websites too. This can tell you a lot about the industry and may give you something to talk about when you get an interview.

Armed with all this information, you'll do better in the interview. When you have accurately targeted the right job and have learned everything you can about the organization, you are far more likely to be successful in the interview process.

WHO ARE YOU?

Figuring out where to look and what satisfies your requirements are only two of the first steps in the search. Another is determining who you are and what kind of worker you'll be. One member of the group had recently completed a Meyers-Briggs Type Indicator (MBTI) assessment. At the conclusion of an MBTI assessment, your personality type is identified by four letters indicating your preferences (**E**xtraversion or **I**ntroversion; **S**ensing or **IN**tuition; **T**hinking or **F**eeling; and **J**udgment or **P**erception).

"So now I've identified my type," she said. "Big deal. How will that help me in my search?" Before I could offer my opinion, other members of the group who had experience with MBTI chimed in with their thoughts.

"It's very valuable," said one. "I hate networking and thought I had to be out there all the time talking to people I hadn't spoken with in years about my needing a job. This was both difficult and embarrassing. Then I completed a Meyers-Briggs survey and found out I was on the introverted side of the axis. It was suggested to me that I could start networking in a much smaller circle, because it was unlikely that I'd be very effective or successful reaching out to strangers. Knowing my communication style made me a much more effective networker and gave me permission to work a smaller set of contacts. I didn't put as much pressure on myself and I didn't feel like a failure." Resisting the scattershot approach made all the difference. Targeting the right people is usually more effective than leaving a string of voicemails with people who are unlikely to return those calls. Figuring out whom to call is the heavy lifting. After you've done that, making the call, the thing you'd dreaded, is easier.

SO, WHAT DO YOU WANT TO DO NOW?

The things you need to determine to focus your search effectively take in every aspect of the job. For instance:

- **Where do you want to work?** In a big city or in the suburbs?

- **How long are you willing to commute?** Do you relish that time alone in the car or look forward to catching up on your reading on the train? For one woman the commute is the only time of day just for her. No kids, no boss, no co-workers. Just her and her mystery novels. What kind of commute works for you?

- **What size firm is right for you?** Do you need to be on a first-name basis with everyone or does the hustle and bustle of a large organization get you going?

- **Does the nature of the business matter?** There are many fields—IT, human resources, operations, customer service—where the skills are the same and transferable and it almost doesn't make that much difference for whom you do it. But some people feel a need to connect with the product of their organization. Some won't work for a company that produces petroleum products, tobacco or alcohol. Others want to work for a "green" organization or feel that their work is making some contribution to society. For some the desire is to work where technology is on the cutting edge. What do you care about? Is it the work you do or for whom you do it? Both?

- **How do you like to be managed?** Are you a more free-wheeling type or do you crave structure? In today's decentralized workplace, you may not have frequent contact with your manager, who may reside in another city or time zone. Can you deal with that? Many organizations are doing away with restrictive policies as they focus mainly on results. Others care as much about how you get the work done as how much you get done. Which is right for you?

- **What about your "personal space"?** Do you want an office or are you okay in a cubicle or "open office"? Are you the person who needs to personalize your desk with lots of distinctive flourishes or will just one picture of the family suffice? Organizations have different views on personalizing your space so this is something to learn in researching a company. Some companies, such as pharmaceuticals and many high-tech companies, are literally sterile atmospheres due to the nature of the work.

- **Are you looking for the same type of work or is it transition time? Are you burnt out in your current field?** Regardless of how successful you might be, some of you are looking for a change because you need to do something different. Also consider if this is a field that is growing or shrinking. You may be the best at what you do but all that may earn you is the right to be the person who turns out the lights when the job or the company disappears.

Once you figure out where you want to work, how you're going to get there, how many people you'll interact with, what the organization produces, how you'll be managed and your preferred physical surroundings, identifying the right company to target is easy!

These are the steps you have to take, the questions you need to answer if you are going to be effective in finding a new job. Before you can find the job, you need to know the kind of job you seek. When I say kind of job I'm talking about lots more than just what you'll be doing from 9:00 to 5:00. It's usually all the other factors that combine to determine if the job is the right one to pursue.

Four

FIGURING OUT
WHAT TO DO NEXT

Can I reinvent myself? Should I?

The last question in Chapter Three addressed the subject of changing to a different field. Making a career shift is one of the options you may be considering. Choosing to transition to an entirely new field is one of the more difficult decisions to make. Sometimes it is a choice and sometimes the decision to switch careers is based on need. If the handwriting is on the wall for your current industry, it makes little sense to continue to pursue opportunities in that field; no matter how good you are at it or how much you love it. Many journalists are feeling that way now and segueing into careers in "new media."

Whether the decision to reinvent yourself is based on choice or need, there are a number of factors to consider. While it may be tempting to make a clean break and start over in a new field, you may be concerned that such a move may not be practical based on your age, location or life situation.

This chapter addresses more specific—and more difficult—questions you need to answer to accurately assess if this is the right move. These questions apply whether you're unemployed or employed. These questions will help you further refine your search if you're considering a career shift. Even if you are not looking to make a change, they are worth asking about your current field.

SHOULD I CHANGE FIELDS?

What makes you think that changing fields will be the answer? Why do you think that changing careers is the right choice now? There are short- and long-term benefits and challenges inherent in this decision.

Short-term, it might be invigorating to explore and get into a new field. It might be a field that's long interested you, but you thought you couldn't afford to leave your job to give it a try. If your job has left you, now could be the time.

One long-term impact is that you will most likely enter this field at a lower level, both hierarchically and salary-wise, than you were at in your previous position. Of course, this might happen even if you stay in your current field. You need to assess the earning potential of this new field. You don't want to leave a sinking ship for one that is taking on water.

There are hard realities to career shifts. Not just the challenges of preparing for and making the move, but the psychological, emotional and financial impact this decision will have. A recent study done at Columbia University of people whose positions were eliminated in the recession of 1980-82 found that 15 to 20 years later, their earnings were about 15-20% lower than those of comparable workers who had not been laid off. Many of these people who were laid off chose to make career changes after being let go. You may not be able to make up the cut in pay you may experience as a result of changing careers. For some, the rewards of new challenges in a new field may outweigh the financial drawbacks. So if you are thinking of changing careers as an option, you need to examine both the short- and long-term effects of this decision.

WHAT'S BOTHERING YOU?

When assessing whether or not to make a move, try to identify the negative triggers you've felt at work. This can help in making the decision whether you need to change industries, change careers or change companies.

If you are unhappy on the job, is it the people you work with or the work you do that bothers you most? What is it that makes it hard to put up with the people you work with? You are going to work with people with whom it is sometimes hard to get along, though hopefully not too often. Why is it that some days these co-workers are minor annoyances and other days they drive you nuts? However the stress may be affecting you, identify what and when you find that it is harder to stay in control, or in good humor. Once you know your triggers, you can work to avoid them. Or at least recognize them and not let them get the best of you. If you find yourself more and more unhappy on the job, this is a clear signal that you need to look for something else to do or somewhere else to do it. If the job is untenable, you will eventually need to move on. Maybe that's why you bought this book.

Let me tell you about Phil. We were discussing whether or not he should consider changing careers. He was extremely frustrated at his current job. Phil was usually at his desk before 8 in the morning. His days often ended after 7:00 PM. "When was the last time you left work when it was still light outside?" I asked. He couldn't remember. And then Phil got angry. He said, "And it's not like the boss will notice; he's usually gone by 5:00 PM." Phil had liked his job as a real estate manager. He'd been doing it for 25 years, but lately it was different. There had been changes in management and he was feeling taken for granted. He needed to pin down what made him feel the way he did.

The next time I saw Phil, he told me he'd come to the realization that he wanted more out of his life than just a job. He'd stopped putting in those ridiculous hours, stopped coming in at 8:00 AM and on Saturdays and Sundays. He had restrung his tennis racquet and joined a gym.

One morning, when he showed up at 8:30, a co-worker asked him if anything was wrong. He seemed different. She asked, "Have you lost something?" He paused and then replied, "No, I think I found something." He had found a path to regain more of his life. He had found that the office could exist without his superhuman efforts. He had found some balance and with it the confidence to consider other career options.

Phil had gotten used to putting in long hours and the office had certainly gotten used to his always being there. But he had gotten away from what he really wanted to do. We explored when he was happy at work. He cited a different job he had held for almost 15 years before he took his current one. That industry had certainly changed over the past 25 years but it was that type of position we started exploring. We needed to determine the feasibility of his return to that function, if not to that industry. We also needed to determine how that job and that industry had changed. It turned out that the situation he fondly remembered no longer existed. We worked together, using many of the questions you'll find in the next section of this chapter, to determine the right path for Phil. After a few weeks, Phil decided to stay in the field he was in, but look for opportunities with other firms. He was able to connect with what he liked to do and realized that going back to his old field was a fantasy. Phil wound up staying in the field he was in, and staying with the same company. But having gone through the process, he changed the way he approached his work so it was not the only thing in his life. He would not have been in a position to make this change, to take greater control of his life, had he not gone through the process of reinvention. In effect, Phil reinvented himself in his current position.

It takes time to prepare to change your life, to change your direction. It's a lot of work. You need to ask yourself some very hard questions and be honest in your answers. The first key is to understand what it is you're looking for. What is it that you really want to do? If you haven't defined what you're looking for, it's impossible to know when you've found it. It's like the saying in *Alice in Wonderland*, "If you don't know where you're going, any road will do."

THE HARD QUESTIONS

The questions found at the end of Chapter Three are ones you need to answer to start your search. If you haven't answered them for yourself yet, nows the time. Once you've finished with them, it's time to dig a little deeper. The next step, especially when considering a more radical move such as changing careers or changing functions within your career, is answering The Hard Questions. These are the soul-searching questions that will help you establish a direction as you reinvent yourself.

- **What do you want from a job?** Are you looking for financial security or is it wealth you desire? Some people just want enough to take care of their family, save for college, and put something away for retirement. Some people seek real wealth. Others want a place where they can feel good about the work or the organization, even if they have to sacrifice some salary. Which is it for you?

- **What do you want from your life?** Do you want to dedicate yourself to your family or are you also invested in the larger community? Perhaps you want to surround yourself with all the newest and best gadgets and things. You need to examine how you define success—by what you do, by the size of your house, by your possessions. Your values help shape who you are. Shouldn't they also shape what job you do?

- **Where are you willing to work?** I know someone who had moved to the suburbs and after 15 years found herself commuting back into a big city. She thought she would dread this but rediscovered how much she loved the vibrancy of a cosmopolitan atmosphere. Someone else I've worked with absolutely hates going into New York City and would rather drive a 90-minute commute. You can't pay him enough to get on a train and subway. Which leads me to…

- **Is the money worth it?** You can take a job that pays more money, but what's the cost? Will the extra money cover the cost of the extended hours for the babysitter, the dry-cleaning for the wardrobe you must maintain, and maybe the therapist you need to start seeing? There's always a trade-off. You're going to have to decide, very often with your spouse or partner, how much money you need and whether the extra money you earn from a higher-paying job is worth it.

- **What are you willing to do?** You may be an accountant or a programmer, but is that what you want to do now? Is it what you want to do next? You are going to have to decide if you want to stay in the field that you are presently in or if you are going to transition to another field.

- **Is there anything you like about your current job or profession?** Something must have attracted you to this function at some point. Can you remember what it was? Was it the desire to help others? Was it the chance to work in a deadline driven environment, which for some is very exciting? Can you, like Phil, reinvent yourself in your current position or profession? Before you make the big change to a whole new career, take the time to see if you can get back to what initially excited you about doing this. For people not willing to make wholesale changes, getting back to your core interests may be the right choice.

- **Are you willing to take the necessary steps to transition to another career or function?** This could mean going back to school, it could mean making a lateral move or even taking a step down your company's organization chart. It may mean a cut in pay, as you'll likely be starting a few rungs down the career ladder. Is this an acceptable trade-off at your current life stage?

- **What kind of organization are you targeting?** Some people use their values to a greater extent than others when choosing an employer. Even in the current labor environment, some candidates are interviewing companies. What kind of company is right for you? Answering this question correctly will go a long way toward helping you find a job that will be more fulfilling than others.

- **Is it the place, the people, or the position?** Determine what's hitting, or more likely hammering, your hot buttons. Is it the company or your co-workers that are driving you nuts? This is no time to make a snap decision. Why are you considering changing careers? This takes careful thought.

- **What are you willing to put up with?** Difficult co-workers? A long commute? A sterile environment? Less money or less security? The perfect job rarely exists. There will always be something wrong with any position you take. One way to make your job less frustrating is to decide ahead of time where or on what you are willing to compromise. When answering these questions it helps to prioritize them from most to least important. You'll then have a better idea of which aspects of the position you're willing to compromise.

- **Are you running to or running from?** Be honest with yourself. Are you considering making a career change just to get away from someone or something at work? Unless you thoughtfully assess what's motivating your desire for a change it's possible that whatever bothered you in the past will follow you in your new career. If we do not learn from the past, we are doomed to repeat it. That's why you're asking yourself all these Hard Questions.

- **What does the perfect job look like *today*?** No short answer here. This question is the sum total of every question we've covered so far. Just remember that what you wanted yesterday may not be what you want today. No matter how long or how hard you've worked to get where you are today, if you've wound up in the wrong place, then it may be time to go in another direction.

IT'S NEVER TOO LATE TO START DOING BETTER

Making a change takes ongoing introspection and revision. Your needs evolve over time. So does your vision of the perfect job. This is the process of reinvention.

Deciding whether or not to stick it out in your current job or career or to switch to another one is an extremely personal decision. There is no simple one-size-fits-all answer. Every answer seems to yield more questions. You need to carefully assess how you feel at work, going to work and on your way home from work. Are you in any way fulfilled by the work you do, or is there an overwhelming emptiness?

The emptiness might come when you're standing on a commuter train platform in the predawn light, realizing that you were on this platform less than 10 hours ago when you came home last night. The emptiness Phil felt when he was closing up at 8 o'clock at night and realizing he hadn't seen another soul for over two hours. The emptiness when you know the night watchman's name but you can't remember your new neighbor's. That's when you start thinking maybe it's time for a change. That's when it may be time to reinvent yourself. I can't tell you. Only you can tell you. If you are honest with yourself, you will know.

Five

CIRCLES OF NETWORKING

I'm no good at talking to strangers!

Get out there and network! Networking is the key to finding a job today! Ninety-nine percent of all openings are filled through word of mouth!

This is what everyone is telling you—yet most people have no idea how to network. Many don't even know what it means. Is it talking to recruiters? Is it talking with friends? Is it talking to strangers? The answer is simply, yes.

Is there a magic formula to networking? If you make X number of calls a day, you'll make a connection with someone who knows someone who can get you an interview, or even better, a job?

If it were that simple, we'd all just be burning through our minutes to get to that magic number.

WHAT IS NETWORKING?

Networking is more than just talking to people. It's talking with a purpose to the people who can help you achieve your goal. In the same way that interviewing is more than merely a conversation, networking is more than just getting your name out there. Interviewing is a conversation with the goal of gathering information. Networking is an exchange of information with the goal of sharing information. As the networker, you want to influence that other person to give you the name of someone to contact, to recommend you to someone, to move you on to the hiring decision-maker or to offer you a job. The person you're trying to network with has a goal too. Are you someone he should recommend? Are you someone who can help him in some way? Will referring you to someone in his network help or potentially damage his own career? There is much to be gained and also something to be lost for both parties when networking.

Determining whom you should be networking with breaks down into three circles: the people you know well; the people you know; and finally the people they know (that is, people you don't know yet).

It looks sort of like this:

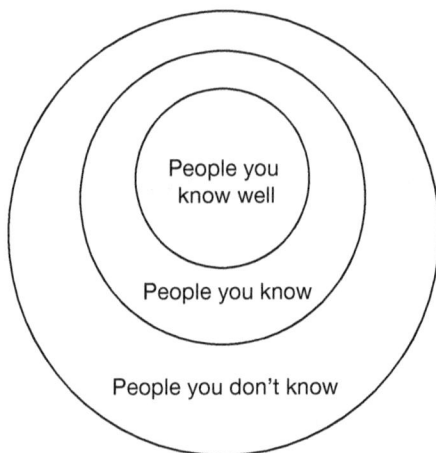

People you know well

People you know

People you don't know

YOUR FIRST CIRCLE

Most of us are willing to talk with the people we know well. This is often known as your Support Network. These are your good friends, family, clergy—people who may already know of your circumstances. Whether you are unemployed, worried about losing your job, or just suffering under a bad boss, these people already know what you're going through. And they're on your side. It's easy to talk with them because you know that they won't judge you, they'll listen and empathize, and they'll most likely make you feel better. And the good news is, this is a great opportunity to practice talking about your situation and to learn how to talk about what you're going through while keeping your emotions in check. The bad news is, these people can't help you find a new job. Think about it. They already know the stress you're under. If they knew of a job for which you were suited, they would have already told you.

This doesn't mean that you shouldn't talk to your first circle. It just means that you shouldn't rely on them. You shouldn't try to convince yourself that by talking with those closest to you that you're networking effectively. You are networking but you're just barely off the ground. To get that new job, you're going to need to soar.

One good use of your first circle is to have them help you do a personal assessment. What do you do best? What are some things that you need to or could do better? What are some areas in which your skills could be best utilized? Talking with your first circle about your skills is great practice and it's easier than asking people for contacts. But ultimately, ask you must and ask you will. You'll need to engage people inside and outside your first circle in conversation about your situation. The people in your first circle want to help you. Make it easy for them by telling them how they can. Ask for honest feedback about your skills and the names of people you can contact to expand your second circle.

In addition to talking about your strengths, skills and ambitions, to get the most out of your first circle you need to ask them who they know who you should be talking to. These aren't necessarily people who can offer you a job, but you're getting closer. Do your first circle contacts know anyone in the industry or function that you're targeting? Do they know anyone who has gone through something similar and came up with a successful strategy? You're trying to tap into their network. You have to ask them for what you want. In sales they say you have to ask for the business. Same thing here. You want the names and phone numbers of people you can talk to who may be able to help you. There's no harm in asking. The worst thing anyone can say is no. Using that sales analogy, "no" is the second-best answer. Obviously you want to hear "yes," whether it's getting a networking contact, an interview, or a job offer. But getting a definitive "no" is good, too, because it allows you to move on to your next contact, your next prospect, your next interview.

Try not to settle for e-mail addresses. It's too easy to ignore e-mail, and a firewall or spam filter may block your message. Active networking means talking to people, and although you may not like it, it often means talking to people you don't know well or don't know at all. Ask the people in your first circle to smooth the road for you. Ask if they'd be willing to contact those people before you do. Would they make a phone call or send an e-mail alerting the person that you'll be calling? That way you are a warm referral rather than a cold call. When you call someone you don't know well and say that so-and-so suggested you call them, they don't know whether so-and-so really did. Your first circle contact's call makes it more likely that they'll take yours.

YOUR SECOND CIRCLE

You're into the second circle. These are people you may know, but not as well as your inner circle. You've met them at parties, or through friends of friends. It takes a moment to remember their names, and you probably don't remember the name of their spouse, but this can't stop you from reaching out and starting a networking conversation.

These conversations are more businesslike and to the point. You both understand the nature of the call or meeting, and while you still have to build some rapport, don't waste the person's time. Be sure to mention your mutual connection—the person from your first circle. Then explain your situation, making it clear that you're reaching out to exchange information, expand your network and let more people know of your talents and availability. You are not calling to ask for a job. If there's a position available in this person's firm or organization that's appropriate for you, your job is to make sure that they make this connection. But if you simply call and ask if they have a job to offer you, the answer will most likely be "no" and that will be the end of the conversation. Or, if it does continue, it will be more strained. Both of you might be thinking at some point, "Why are we still talking?" You're calling to let the person know of your availability, the skills that you offer and to ask for further referrals. Who do they know that you should be contacting? Earlier I said that no is the second-best answer, and it is—but with second circle contacts you want to have an open-ended conversation rather than a closed one.

The conversation you have with second and third circle contacts are often called informational interviews. Put the person at ease by explaining right off the bat that you're not calling to find out if he or she has a job for you. You're calling to gather information about her firm, function or field. This will relax your contact, since she won't feel pressure to come up with something. You just want to talk. Of course, what you really want is to make sure that she sees you in a new light. You hope she will start to think about how you may be able to help her company or link you to someone else she knows who may have a need for someone with your skills.

When you speak with this contact, in person or on the phone, have a few prepared questions. There's a list of suggested questions at the end of this chapter. Your first goal is to get the person talking. Having her describe her own career arc is often a good way to get started. Furthermore, it's an easy place to start. She still may not be sure of why you want to talk with her, so make it easy for her to look and feel successful. Just be sure you bring the conversation around to your own needs at some point.

I remember an informational interview that I had very early

in my own transition to human resources. Through my network, I secured a meeting with a senior HR manager at a financial services firm. He kept me waiting 15 minutes and started off by saying that he had only a half hour to give me and we had already cut into that. I asked one or two questions to put him at ease—and he was off to the races. I didn't say another word for the next 45 minutes. At the conclusion of our meeting, he said that he thought I was a very intelligent fellow who would go far in this field. I was curious to know what he based his opinion on since I had said virtually nothing during the entire meeting, so I asked. His reply? "You're a very thorough interviewer." I learned a lot about being a good listener that day, but I realized that I had done pitifully little to market myself to this potential contact. I had only completed half of my objective.

At some point, you have to direct the conversation back toward your own skills, abilities and talents. Do this diplomatically, because you're not on a job interview. Be careful not to oversell yourself. When you talk about your accomplishments, or the things you hope to achieve in your next position, think of this as information he needs. Help him to think of you as a marketable product. Tipping someone else off to your availability would be a real feather in his cap. Make him see the benefit of referring you to someone who may be able to offer you a job.

Interviews are conversations that have the goal of gathering information. The information you want is the names and phone numbers of people he knows who you should be talking to. You want to tap into his network and you want him to be happy to provide the names. He will be giving you something very precious to use: his reputation. People don't refer people who will reflect poorly on them. You have no more than 30 or 40 minutes, and sometimes even less, to convince him that you're worth referring. Be prepared to conclude the informational interview by getting the information that you need to achieve your goal. Don't be embarrassed by asking outright for it. Ideally at the beginning of the meeting you set the stage properly so that at the end it seems only natural for him to give you the names of a few contacts from his network.

YOUR THIRD CIRCLE

Your meetings with your third circle of contacts, people you don't know, will be similar in many ways to your second circle meetings. At this point, though, you will be getting closer to people who have jobs to offer. Some third-circle contacts will be nothing more than additional network contacts, but some will have vacancies in their organizations. That may be why your second-circle contact referred you in the first place.

This is why you have to get to that third circle. This is where the jobs are. You may get lucky and hit on something in the second or even the first circle, but networking solely in your inner circles is like digging in an oil well that has run dry. You'll wind up covered in dust with nothing to show for it.

You've probably heard that people find new jobs through word of mouth, and it's true—estimates are that more than 60% of all jobs are filled this way. Your task now is to find those people who have the jobs that need to be filled. Your first and second circle contacts can lead you to people you don't know and introduce and recommend you to them. That's how it's supposed to, and often does, work. But not always. When it doesn't, that's when emotions creep back in and make networking harder.

People often become depressed when they're looking for jobs because they think they've exhausted all their options. They say to me, "I've spoken to everyone I know!" I reply, "But you haven't spoken with everyone you don't know."

I was once trying to buy a house in the suburbs. We'd been looking at houses for months and were already in contract to sell our apartment. We hadn't even found a house we wanted to put a bid on. My wife was getting just a wee bit frantic. I was equally nervous, but I said to her, "The house we are going to buy isn't even on the market yet. But it will be, and when it is we'll be ready." Less than ten days later we did find a new listing. We looked at the house the first day it was on the market, made an offer that afternoon and had an accepted offer that evening. We were ready to move because we had already done all our legwork. We knew it was right.

Looking for a job is in many ways like looking for a new home. You're going to see a lot of places you couldn't imagine walking into everyday. You're going to see some wonderful places that you can't afford. When it's a house, you sometimes can't afford it because it costs too much. When it's a job, it may seem to be a wonderful opportunity but you can't afford it because it pays too little. You're going to meet lots of people you may never see again, and you're going to suffer a lot of rejection. Ultimately you're going to find a house or a job. Maybe you'll find it by combing through the real estate listings or on the job boards. Maybe you'll work with a real estate broker or career counselor. And just maybe someone is going to tip you off to someone who knows someone who is thinking of moving or is looking for someone just like you. If you've done your networking, whether in real estate or your job search, you'll be ready.

Talking with people you don't know is the hardest kind of networking—the kind most people will do anything to avoid. But if you become skilled at this degree of networking, it will work to your advantage for the simple reason that so many other people are loath to do it. It's been said that in this world, there are talkers and there are doers. Be one of the doers: you will find it is far less crowded. In fact, the more you network outside of your immediate circle, the more adept you'll become at it, which will get you that much further ahead of your competition. The people you contact, though they won't know you, will be more willing to talk or meet with you because of the way you present yourself. You're confident, you're organized, and you're not going to waste their time. You've come in with a purpose, a focus and a direction. People like that. Think about the last time someone asked you a favor. If they hemmed and hawed and beat around the bush, did you get frustrated? You may have thought, "Just spit it out. Go ahead and ask me!" Most people prefer to work with people who are direct and businesslike, especially in a business setting. At this level of networking, this is a business meeting, even if it's framed as an informational interview. You should walk in with an agenda, a plan and a desired outcome; whether it's another contact, a job lead or even the possibility of being considered for a job with that person's organization. Your goal is not to be a professional interviewer, but at this point you will be pretty good at it, and that's the key. And the only way to get good at interviewing is to interview. Your practice in the first and second circles has prepared you for the major leagues of interviewing. You're in the third circle, and now you're playing for keeps. You're not playing with house money as you were in the first circle. It's real now; there may be a job on the line and because of your preparation you're not going to blow it. You're going to follow the steps of a good interview and you will nail it.

INFORMATIONAL INTERVIEWS

Here's an outline of what an informational interview, either in person or on the phone, might look like. You may not touch on every step and sometimes your time with the contact is condensed. You might also find that your interview follows a different pattern, but certain elements are essential: a solid opening, some probing questions; describing what you have to offer; asking for additional contacts; and closing strong, including the follow-up "thank you."

Here are the steps of an informational interview meeting:
- Thank the person for his time and for agreeing to see you.
- Explain your current situation. This may be that you are unemployed and looking for work; looking for a new opportunity in your current field or function; or looking to make a change to a new field or function.

- Explain why you're interested in talking with him.
- Ask a few open-ended questions about his background and experience. These may include "How did you get started in this field?"; "What interests you about it?"; "How do you see the field evolving over the next few years?"
- Explain why you are interested in exploring your options.
- Describe some successes in your current or last position, ideally ones that can relate to the field or function you're investigating. Be sure to describe your work ethic, not just what you did.
- Explain how your past success translates into potential success.
- Ask for recommendations about how to learn more about the field or function. Ask what you might consider doing next.
- Ask if he would be comfortable sharing the names and phone numbers of people you could or should contact. If he does give you names and numbers, ask if he would be willing to contact them to let them know that you will be reaching out. A warm referral gets a response far more often than a cold call. If he opts not to give you names and numbers, ask if he would be comfortable giving your name to people in his network. Ask for the names of whom he will contact. Assure him that you will not try to contact these people; you simply want the names so that you can recognize them when you get a call. Your credibility and integrity is on the line here, and so is the reputation of whoever helped you get this meeting. Resist the temptation to call the people whose names he gives you if he prefers you don't.
- Thank him for his time and ask if there is anything you can do for him (short of washing his car).
- Get his business card and give him yours.
- After the meeting, send a thank you note (not an e-mail). The note does not need to be handwritten. This is both a

thank you and a reminder of: your availability, your interest and what he agreed to do for you.

NETWORKING QUESTIONS

Below is a list of helpful networking questions. You won't use all these questions but pick the ones that work best for you, your field and the person you're meeting or speaking with.

- What companies do you respect?
- Do you know anyone whose skill set is similar to mine?
- Do you know anyone whose function is similar to mine?
- Are there certain fields or functions in which you see a lot of opportunity?
- What fields or functions are shrinking or disappearing altogether?
- How has your profession changed over the past few years?
- What obstacles have you had to overcome in your career?
- What changes do you think may occur over the next few years?
- What trade or professional organizations do you belong to?
- What value have you gotten from being a member?
- Are there any volunteer opportunities with this organization?
- How did you secure your last position?
- How much lateral or vertical mobility is there in your function?
- Tell me about things you do to keep in touch with your network.
- Who do you consider an expert in this field?
- What skills are critical for success in your field or function?
- While both are obviously important, which do you think is more important for success in this industry, the hard, technical skills or the more strategic, or soft, skills?
- Where can I learn more about this field or function?
- Now that you know a little bit about me, what do you think are some good fields to consider?

- In what functions have people with my skills been successful?
- Are there any programs you recommend to learn more about your field or function?
- Is there anything I've neglected to ask you that it would be helpful to know?
- Would it be alright to contact you if I have additional or follow-up questions?

Six

FOLLOWING UP

How long should I wait?

How soon should I call after I send in my resume? This is one of the most common questions I hear. My favorite response is, "What are you waiting for?" Usually people don't want to appear too anxious. They say they want to give the recruiter a chance to go over the resume. Or maybe they don't know why they're waiting. Maybe someone told them that you should wait a week before following up on a resume submission although I can't imagine why. It's not like you mailed it and you have to wait three days for the post office to get it there.

TIMING YOUR FOLLOW-UP

I remember when people used to calculate the right day to mail their resume. "The job was listed on Sunday. I need to compose my cover letter. It will take two or three days to get it there. I don't want my resume to arrive on a Friday or Monday so I will mail the resume on the Thursday after I see the ad in the paper so it will arrive on the recruiter's desk on Tuesday. Then I'll follow up with a call later that week." For those of you who only entered the job market in the last ten years, I'll wait while you recover from shock. But that's what it used to be like to find a job in what were referred to as the "Classifieds." I think that may be where the myth of not calling for a week or so after submission began. But think about today.

You submit your resume and cover e-mail with the click of a mouse. Your resume goes into an Applicant Tracking System that spits out an automated response ("Do not respond to this e-mail," it warns.) And if you have the correct combination of skills (or at least the correct combination of key words embedded) your resume will be forwarded on to a screener who will call you and do his or her best to eliminate you from consideration. All this before your resume is even seen by a recruiter and you're worrying about when to call?

Here's something that I picked up recently: A recruiter said that he never contacts anyone immediately upon receiving a resume, even if he's interested in the person. He waits a week. If he has not received a follow-up call or e-mail from the person in that first week, he tosses the resume no matter how good it looks. Initiative and perseverance are two of the qualities that he is looking for in his people. It is critical to success in his organization, and if the applicant says in the cover letter (or e-mail) that he'll follow up but doesn't, he disqualifies them.

I know we all worry how often or how soon to follow up. In this case, it's never too soon. When you say that you're giving the recruiter time, or you don't want to appear too anxious, maybe you're just ducking the possibility of rejection. Maybe you're just procrastinating for who knows what reason—and heaven knows there are plenty.

MAKE THE CALL!

The bottom line is, if you want the job, make the call. Nobody likes rejection. Nobody likes making endless calls and leaving countless messages. I know one woman who imagines the recruiter listening to her message, slapping his forehead and saying, "Oh no, not her again! Won't she ever get the message? Can't she figure out that I'm not interested and I'm not going to call her?" But this is not often the case. Recruiters are often overwhelmed with resumes, messages and calls. The more you keep calling, the more likely you are to be the one person who gets through. As Wayne Gretzky said, "You miss 100% of the shots you don't take." Take your shot. Make the call.

How many times should you call to follow up? When do you accept the fact that maybe they don't want you and cross them off your call list?

Renowned speaker and sales expert Brian Tracy says you find success on the fifth call. The problem is, most people get fed up and frustrated after about three calls. So the difference between success and failure is two calls. Do you think you have the energy, the perseverance, the gumption to make two more calls? If I told you that you would get through to a live person on the fifth call, but not the third or the fourth, would you keep calling? Of course you would.

Unfortunately, I can't guarantee success on the fifth call. The recruiter will not see your number on the caller ID, know it's your fifth call, and pick up the phone saying, "Congratulations on your perseverance! You have worn me down and won the prize!" It doesn't work that way. I recently got someone on the phone and booked a series of workshops that I'll be presenting for her company. This was someone for whom I had already successfully presented workshops. And I got through to her on the ninth call. Can you imagine if I was cold calling? Whether it's the fifth call or the ninth call, if you feel you're a viable candidate for the position, keep calling.

Every article you read that tells you that this is a down economy is correct. Does that mean you shouldn't call? Of course not. Yes, the economy is in a slump but that does not mean that there isn't work that needs to get done. People are still moving from one job to another, just not as often, as quickly or as easily as in better times. A survey done by CareerBuilder in the last two months of 2008 said that almost 20% of employed people were looking to change jobs in 2009. Companies are still hiring, just not as many and far more carefully. But there are literally thousands of jobs listed on the Internet and some of them must be real.

ARE THE JOBS I SEE LISTED FOR REAL?

One member of the Job Support Group has a particular reason for not pursuing any postings he sees on any of the Internet job boards. He insists that all the listings on the Internet are there because they have to be listed, but the jobs have actually been filled internally. He thinks the postings are solely for compliance purposes. Well, some of the positions posted on job boards are there to keep the company in compliance with federal or state regulations. Your task as a jobseeker is to find the real ones. Do your research. Is the company announcing reductions at the same time it's hiring? This is sometimes an indicator that the job is real because even while a company is downsizing, there will always be jobs of a critical nature that cannot be left vacant. As counterintuitive as this sounds, consider applying for the job with the company that just announced a reduction in force. This must be a job that must be filled even while the company is reducing elsewhere. The posting is simply an indicator that the company does not have, or doesn't think it has, the talent internally.

Blind ads, ones that do not list a company, are less likely to bear fruit. These are the ones that often are listed for compliance purposes. However, sometimes companies that are reducing staff prefer to use blind ads so that they don't send the wrong message to recently exited employees. How does it look when a company that just laid off a thousand or more workers is listing ads for new hires? Pretty confusing. Companies sometimes use blind ads to hide the fact that they are hiring during a layoff. Therefore you shouldn't just ignore any ad that doesn't list a company, or is listed by a recruiting firm.

Blind ads are often overlooked by jobseekers because of their ambiguity. But sometimes organizations use blind ads because they want to find people who really want to do this function and are not simply attracted to the company. You have—or should have—target companies. These are the companies that you'd like to work for based on their culture, their product, their location or some other reason. Whenever you see a posting from this company, you will want to apply. Sometimes in your zeal to get into the company you overlook the fact that you are only marginally qualified for the job. Organizations use blind ads to discourage people who are only trying to get a foot in the door and aren't really interested in investing a few years performing the responsibilities of the advertised position. No company wants to fill a position only to have to fill it again in less than a year. Blind ads are a way to find those candidates who are truly interested in doing a specific job.

In addition, if you're doing your research and your homework, it is possible to take the wrapping off a blind ad. If the ad alluded to a "Major soft-drink and snack food provider just north of New York City" you have pretty good idea that it's talking about Pepsico. If the company bills itself as the "leading global food service retailer" and they're just west of Chicago, you're going to McDonald's. A big part of determining which ads to pursue is connecting the dots of industry, location and activity. Pay attention to which pharmaceutical company has just won FDA approval for a new drug. Then if you see an ad for pharmaceutical sales positions in central New Jersey, you'll have a good idea which of the many companies based there it is. You can waste a lot of time with blind ads, or you can take the time to decipher them. The key is to determine which are the ones most likely to bear fruit.

KEEP FOLLOWING UP

Make the call. Don't assume that just because you posted a resume online that you're done. Submitting a resume is only the first step. Nobody ever got a job just because they submitted a resume. That's only the first step in a long series of steps that you will take during your search. If you're lucky the resume will generate a call. That's all it's supposed to do. The call is to get you an in-person interview, very often with human resources, and the purpose of the HR or screening interview is to get you to the hiring manager (or not), and sometimes she isn't even the final decision maker.

Earlier I said that organizations are being more careful in their hiring. This often means multiple rounds of interviews. When a company is hiring so few people, they want to get it right. They can't, or think they can't, afford a mistake. So expect to be put through the wringer of multiple interviews. Interviews may be with other managers and sometimes with the people who will be your colleagues. There are so many candidates out there today that having the right mix of skills, background and experience is just your ticket of admission. The actual hiring decision is based not on what you can do, but on how you do it. The word "chemistry" is overused but that is what a lot of hiring decisions are based on. The person who gets the offer is often the one the hiring manager feels will work in a way that is consistent with the way people get things done in that organization.

You may be thinking, "So it has nothing to do with my skills and ability? It all comes down to luck and chemistry?" But that's not true. Without the skills, accomplishments and experience represented on your resume, you never would have gotten past the screener. Don't sabotage your chance now that you've done all the research and preparation. Don't make excuses for not pursuing every viable lead.

You can't afford to give up. If you are unemployed, there are few better uses for your time than to make the calls. If you are trapped in a dead-end job with little or no future, making the call is the first step toward finding something more fulfilling. If your organization may be merging with another or is a takeover target, you can't afford to wait until the music stops to see if you still have a seat.

Shakespeare knew the value of following up and persistence over 400 years ago when he wrote in *King Lear*, "Nothing can come of nothing: speak again."

Make the call.

Seven

DEALING WITH
THE BLACK HOLE

What to do when recruiters
don't return calls

When recruiters don't return our calls, we get may upset, depressed or indignant. At my Job Support Group meetings this is one of the most frequently cited causes of frustration. It happens at all stages of the search. One member refers to applying online as sending his resume into the black hole of cyberspace. If you're fortunate enough to have a phone number to call to follow up, you are almost guaranteed to get voicemail. As stated in the previous chapter, you have to make that call, and usually more than once. You can't let the frustration, anger or depression you may be feeling seep into or overtake your tone of voice.

Even more frustrating is when you have succeeded in landing an interview and after the meeting the recruiter or hiring manager doesn't return your calls. As one member put it, "If they don't call me in response to a resume that's one thing. That's just a piece of paper. But they've met me. I'm a human being, not just a name on a resume. Now it's personal! Where's the simple human decency? Why can't they just tell me what's going on? I'm a professional. If the answer is no, then the answer is no. I can deal with that but don't leave me hanging by my thumbs for weeks on end!" Sound familiar?

Take a deep breath. Try not to take it personally. There are a million reasons, many of which have nothing to do with you, that could be stopping the person from getting back to you. There's a hiring freeze but they can't tell you that because it would reflect poorly on the company. They've been pulled off this search because a more critical one came up. The hiring manager is on vacation so the recruiter can't get in touch with them to review the list of candidates. In each case the recruiter has a perfectly good reason not to call you back, but is absolutely still interested in speaking with you when the time comes. It's just that the time is not now.

Now if you're out there looking for a job, none of this does much to make you feel better. You need a job. You're in limbo. You don't know if they're still interested. Or if it's earlier in the process, you're not sure if they've even gotten your resume and would it be so hard just to acknowledge receipt of the darn thing?!?

I HOPE SHE'S ALRIGHT!

Whenever someone doesn't get back to me, for whatever reason, but especially when I don't know the reason, here's what I do to try to alleviate the stress.

I say to myself, "Gee, I hope she's alright. I hope she's not sick or something." If you got a call from a recruiter two weeks after you had e-mailed a resume and she told you that she couldn't call back sooner because she'd been laid up in the hospital, you wouldn't be angry with her. You'd express concern for her health and you'd be happy to hear from her. Somewhere in the back of your mind you might even be angry with yourself for having been so mad at the recruiter. She couldn't call you back. See, you got all stressed out for nothing.

Now this may sound rather Pollyanna-ish, but there's a very good reason to take this approach. During those two weeks when you don't hear anything from the recruiter, you're probably calling and leaving voicemails for her as you follow up on the posting. They go something like this:

First call: "Hi Edie, this is Ron Katz. I e-mailed my resume to you three days ago for the HR Generalist position. Just following up to see if we can set up an interview. Please call me at 212-555-5783. Look forward to hearing from you."

Second call: "Hi, Edie, Ron Katz again. Just following up on that resume you got last week. At least I hope you got it. Give me a call at 212-555-5783 if you need me to send you another. I'd be happy to. Really hope to hear from you soon."

Third call: "Hi, Edie. Ron Katz here. Just checking to see if you've filled that Generalist slot yet. Haven't heard from you and wondering if you've started setting up interviews. I'd love to meet with you. Just call me at 212-555-5783 and we can set one up. Please call. Thanks."

Fourth call (and you really debated whether it's even worth it to keep calling at this point): "Edie, Ron Katz here. Hate to be a pest, but I haven't heard anything from you about that HR Generalist job, and I was wondering if it was still open. I am very interested in the job. If you can, please call me at 212-555-5783 if it's not too much trouble. Or at least let me know if the job's been filled so I can stop bugging you. Ron Katz. 212-555-5783. Call me."

Fifth (and likely final) call: "Edie, I guess you've already filled the HR job, or maybe you're going in a different direction, as they say. Anyway, I would've appreciated a call or e-mail so I had some idea of what was going on. If you still want to get in touch with me, the number is 212-555-5783. Call me, or, whatever."

PUT A SMILE IN YOUR VOICE

The way you feel about the person starts to infect your attitude, your behaviors and your tone of voice every time you call. And the more calls you make, the more frustrated you get. The key is to not let that frustration infect your voice. I once worked as the HR manager for a customer service group. I noticed when walking through the department that there was a little mirror attached to the top of every computer monitor facing the person sitting at that terminal.

The customer service manager explained that she wanted people to be able to see themselves and to see the expression on their faces. She wanted them "to put a smile in their voice." I'm sure as you read the five telephone messages above you could "hear" the tone creeping into my voice. If you were the recruiter getting those messages, how disposed would you be to want to call that person back? Not likely I'm sure. This is why it's important not to get exasperated with recruiters when they don't call back as promptly as you'd like. And why it's so important to keep a positive frame of mind when you call them. April Callis, of Springboard Consulting, recommends standing when you call people. Her research shows that it will help you to be more alert and focused. It can also give you more energy and that will come through in your voice too.

A while ago my family had been invited to a wedding and I had to buy "dress pants" for my two sons, who at the time were ages 10 and 8. The affair was in mid-September. We selected the clothes in late August and were at the clothing store in early September to pick them up after tailoring. This was the same time that just about everyone within 10 miles was at this popular children's clothing store buying "Back to School" clothes. The store was mobbed and tensions were pretty high. Not many parents look forward to going shopping with their children for school clothes, and the kids aren't too happy about it either. The boys tried on their pants and found that both pair had been hemmed to the proper length for my younger son, meaning that they were at about mid-shin on my older boy. The wedding was the following weekend and there were no more pants of this type in the store. This was a prime opportunity for me to join in the cacophony of voices at Customer Service.

I had seen about ten people ahead of me on line call the manager everything but a child of God and seen him give it back to them the same way. Lots of, "Nothing can be done. Store credit. Next!" I knew that this would not be a workable solution for me. When it was my turn at the desk I smiled and explained the predicament and asked. "How can we rectify this?" The manager paused and said, "Let me call the store in the next town." It was still pretty crazy in the store and the manager had to wait on hold while the other store checked their inventory. While he was on hold his staff kept asking him questions and other customers kept shouting at him. When the answer came back that the other store had no stock, before I had a chance to say a word he said, "Let me check the store in Jersey, they're a lot bigger."

Now my boys were starting to get antsy. I had promised them that all we had to do was pick up the pants and we'd be on our way. When they started whining I said (loudly enough for the manager, and others, to hear), "The manager is working very hard to get you the pants you need. We just have to give him the time to do his job. He's trying very hard to help you." It turned out the larger store in Jersey was going to have to call him back; it would be a few minutes. But he'd seen my younger son hanging off me and heard what I'd said. Before he went to help the other customers in line he asked my son what his favorite team was. My son told him and within one minute two baseball caps appeared for my sons. They stopped fidgeting so much. About five minutes later, the Jersey store called back. Bingo! They had the pants! They could overnight them to this store, they already had the measurements and I could pick them up that Friday, the night before the wedding. We were saved. I thanked the manager profusely for all he had done for us. As I was about to leave the counter he said, "Y'know, you boys got caps but Dad shouldn't leave empty-handed." He asked me my size and I left with a polo shirt from the store. Plus he said he would refund the cost of the tailoring on one pair of pants for my inconvenience. We all left the store in pretty good spirits, especially my younger son who had gotten a cap from his favorite team!

It would have been very easy for me to get steamed as I waited in line. I could have prepared myself to be treated badly by the manager and worked up a pretty good lather as I waited my turn at the Customer Service Desk. But that wouldn't have served my purpose, which was to get pants for my boys to wear at the wedding.

REMEMBER THE BIG PICTURE

When calling a recruiter to follow up on a resume, try to imagine the day they must be having. Bombarded with resumes. Harassed by managers. Frustrated by candidates. Be the person the recruiter wants to talk with. Put that smile in your voice, especially when you're leaving a message, and you're more likely to get a return call. It's very tempting to let pent-up frustration come out on the one live recruiter you finally make contact with. There's a part of you that may want to let this one person get all the anger you feel toward all those recruiters who haven't returned your calls or responded to your resume. Resist this temptation, regardless of how they treat you, when you finally get a living breathing person on the phone. Even if they're giving you the brush, you want, and likely need, to keep this person in your network. Using this conversation as your opportunity to get back at all the lowlifes who ignored you does not get you one inch closer to your goal. Responding professionally may. Dealing with adversity is one of the behavioral characteristics or intangibles so much in demand in today's workplace. When you lose, don't lose the lesson. So this time you lost. You didn't get the job, or even an interview. What are you going to take from this interaction and, more important, what are you going to leave the recruiter with? Hopefully with a positive impression so you'll be considered for the next opening or referral.

The next time someone doesn't return your call, don't get mad. It doesn't do you any good and it probably hurts your chance at even getting an interview, much less a job. There's nothing to be gained by giving the recruiter attitude, and there is much to be lost. Try to give her the benefit of the doubt and be sure to put yourself in the best frame of mind when you call.

Try to think that maybe she has a broken leg and can't call cause she's in a cast up to her hip, in intense pain and drugged up with medication. At least that's how I like to picture people who don't return my calls.

Eight

YOU HAVE AN INTERVIEW!

Now what do I do?!?

Interviews, once you get to them, are both wonderful and terrifying. It's your goal, it's what you've been working toward, hoping for, praying for. And now you have one. Oh my God, I haven't interviewed in over ten years! What do I do now???

Take a breath.

While getting the interview is no small feat these days, it is not the goal. It is one of the milestones on the way to your goal, which is getting an offer and successfully landing a job. But the interview is a critical step along the way. This is your first opportunity to speak in person with a live human being who actually works at the company you've targeted and might be involved in making a decision that will affect your whole life and whether or not your kids can go to college!!!

Take another breath.

The interview is part of the process of getting a job. It is virtually impossible to get a job without going through at least one and often several interviews either face-to-face, on the phone, or over the Internet. This is the next part of your training in how you are going to influence the decision makers to realize that you are indeed the best person for the job.

Interviews, when done well by a trained and competent interviewer, are not the painful inquisitions we may have experienced in the past. They are still sometimes as ambiguous as the clues in an acrostic puzzle, but if the interviewer is prepared and has a clear understanding of what skills he or she is seeking, the interview can be a lively exchange about a topic you hopefully are well prepared to talk about. And that topic is YOU!

There are lots of different types of questions that you will be asked in the interview, and there is a clear structure to a well-conducted interview. One tip-off that the interviewer has not prepared fully is if you are asked that age-old question, "Tell me about yourself" early in the interview. As soon as you hear that, you can relax. Because you can safely assume that you know as much about interviewing as the person sitting in the room with you.

THE INTERVIEW STRUCTURE

There are generally five phases to the interview. These are:
- the introductory portion or icebreaker;
- the nuts and bolts—basic information about the position and the company;
- the probing preliminary questions you will be asked;
- an opportunity for you to share information that you wish to bring up or questions that you want to ask; and finally,
- the closing.

You must recognize the signals for each phase so that you are best able to respond. Understanding the phases of the interview will also make it easier to give the interviewer the information he or she needs. And the interview does not move from one phase to the next in lockstep as described above. Sometimes the interview jumps all over the place. Sometimes parts of the interview are skipped completely.

ICEBREAKERS

This is the easiest part of the interview to recognize because it comes at the beginning. Interviewers who do not properly set the stage are doing themselves, their organizations and their candidates a huge disservice. You will recognize this phase because this is when the interviewer is making "small talk." Asking about the weather, perhaps offering you a cup of coffee and generally just getting to know you a little. But there is nothing small about small talk. In point of fact, this is when the interviewer is forming his or her first impression of you, so this is the first critical juncture of the interview. First impressions are important because it is very hard for some people to shake them. Have you ever walked out of an interview thinking to yourself, "I never had a chance. They just didn't like me." This was the devious first impression at work. As strange as it may seem, the clothes you wore, the color of your hair, your cologne or perfume may have made up the interviewer's mind before you had a chance to answer a single question. A good interviewer will defer judgment until she has learned more about you. First impressions are powerful things, and there are steps you can take to make yours a good one.

Your job during the introductory portion is to say enough to keep your interviewer glad that she brought you in, but not say anything that could sink your candidacy before the interview is fully under way. It's a great idea to let the interviewer do a lot of the talking in this stage. Remember, many recruiters are as nervous as their candidates during interviews. For human resource representatives in large organizations, she is only as good as her last hire, even after hundreds of interviews. So she has a lot riding on how well she does and how much she learns about you in the 20 or 30 or 40 minutes that she spends with you.

Pay close attention to the interviewer's behavior. Is she calm or scattered? Does her mind seem to be elsewhere or is she completely focused on the conversation you're having? The interviewer is supposed to be making you feel at ease but sometimes it's just the other way round. Do everything you can to create that calm atmosphere for the important exchange of information that is about to take place. Be attentive to her moods, but if she is frenetic, that is not the rhythm you want to mirror. Be the island of calm in the storm of her day. Recruiters are all too familiar with meeting desperate people who need a job badly. That may be you too, but if you don't show it you will appear more confident and employable. Look around the room in which you are meeting. Are there any points of commonality? You don't want to get into a personal conversation about children or families, but if you are meeting in the recruiter's office, look for a diploma that tells you where she went to college, or perhaps an award that she has received. Show that you are perceptive and sensitive to your surroundings.

NUTS AND BOLTS

Many recruiters like to segue from the introductory portion of the interview to telling you a little bit about the organization and the position for which you are interviewing. This is a golden opportunity for you to learn some unvarnished truths about how the organization really works. Listen carefully as the interviewer explains how the organization functions, what is valued and what the culture is like. Cues that you are entering this phase of the interview often sound like: "Let me tell you a little bit about how we operate around here" or "Let me fill you in on the specific duties of the position." The good news is that many inexperienced interviewers tend to go overboard in this part of the interview. It's not that they will tell you trade secrets or proprietary information about the company, but they may inadvertently telegraph the answers to later questions. If, as he is talking, he frequently refers to the project teams, task forces or committees on which you may be involved, then you know to focus on your team spirit when describing yourself. Look for opportunities to stress how successful you have been when working with others. Does it sound as if the people who are most looked up to in this organization are the "lone rangers," the innovators, the free spirits? If so, then you want to make sure that you play up your initiative and creativity.

Don't worry that you aren't getting to say much during this phase of the interview. You'll get your chance later when you are asked questions. Right now your best tactic is to listen, absorb and learn as much as you can about the company you hope to join.

More skilled interviewers will often save this phase of the interview until after they have had the opportunity to ask you questions about your skills and experience. If the interviewer plunges ahead into probing questions after a few minutes of rapport building at the outset of the interview, so be it. But be sure to listen when the interviewer does proceed to talk about the organization. An effective way to use the information he gives you is in the "Sharing" portion of the interview, when he asks you if you have anything to add or if you have any questions. This is a great chance to show that you have been paying attention and frame a question about something he just told you about the organization.

One additional thing to note about the Nuts and Bolts phase: this is the most frequently bypassed portion of the interview. Particularly if the recruiter is running behind and has a waiting room full of candidates to see, this is the easiest part of the interview to skip. Especially if you have not already demonstrated that you are a viable candidate, he may not bother to take the time to offer information about the company. But take heart, just because you aren't given any information about the inner workings of the organization does not mean that you blew the interview. It may just be that the interviewer is simply trying to shave a few minutes off each interview to get back on schedule. Sometimes recruiters are under intense pressure to see a certain number of people in a day. Some organizations place a higher priority on getting through all the candidates than really conducting thorough and effective interviews. If you sense that the recruiter is very conscious of the time passing, tailor your interview style to show that you are a good fit for the organization. Make sure to make your answers succinct and to the point. Don't go rambling on about your first job back in high school. Adjust your responses to show that you can blend in well with a deadline-driven, every-second-counts atmosphere. If you do this, your style of answering may carry more weight than the content of your answers.

PROBING QUESTIONS

One of the most effective ways to gauge how to answer an interviewer's questions is to be prepared for the kinds of questions you'll likely hear. And there are different types of questions you'll be asked during the interview. Recognizing them will help you enormously toward giving both the right answer as well as the right kind of answer. Sometimes the recruiter is asking you to describe some particular incident from your past, perhaps how you responded in a specific situation. Other times you may be asked to think more creatively as to how you would respond if you found yourself in that spot. And at other times you may be asked to demonstrate your critical and analytical skills. One of the keys to answering well is taking the time to be sure that you are providing the information the recruiter really wants and not using the opportunity to go off on a tangent about the time you were planting trees with your college's environmental club. Not that I have anything against trees.

The four primary types of questions are:
- Broad-based
- Hypothetical work situations
- Compare/contrast
- Behavior-based

All of these are designed to probe your background, your experience and the depth of your skills and knowledge. Each goes about it in a different way, but the goal is the same. Are you a viable candidate who will be able to get the job done? This needs to be your focus throughout the interview. You need to demonstrate beyond the shadow of a doubt that you can produce the outcomes the organization expects of whoever is hired to fill this position.

There is a fifth type of question, sometimes called the Abstract or the Brainteaser style of question, popularized by Microsoft. While almost every interviewer will use some combination of the four types of questions listed above, not every employer uses brainteaser-style questions.

There is a fuller explanation of the different types of questions, as well as how to recognize them and best answer them, in the next chapter. The probing questions portion of the interview is the most important time you'll spend with the recruiter. Your answers to the questions you are asked will form the basis of the interviewer's opinion of you as a candidate. It is critically important that you listen carefully to each question to be sure that you are answering the questions asked. Take your time when answering. You will not be evaluated on how quickly you answer, but on how well you do so.

In a good interview, the recruiter is not setting out landmines in order to trip you up. Instead, an interview is a conversation with the goal of gathering, and sharing, information. Every question is an opportunity to test not just your subject matter expertise but also your listening and communication skills. The more conversational the interviewer makes your time together, the more information she is going to get out of you. Make sure that you clearly understand what is being asked and then respond appropriately. If you are not sure, it's okay to ask for clarification. It's also okay to ask for a moment to collect your thoughts if you will need more than five or so seconds before you answer.

SHARING

When you reach the Sharing stage, you may be tempted to relax. And perhaps you can if you've done your homework in advance and are prepared for what's next. You may be in the home stretch, but that doesn't mean the interviewer will hand the reins of the interview over to you and gives you an opportunity to take the interview wherever you want it to go. Absolutely not! Think carefully about what you want to say if you are asked "Do you have any questions for me?" or perhaps "Is there anything else you'd like to tell me about that I haven't asked you?"

Have a few questions ready to ask the interviewer. Scanning the company's website is a great way to do research on what you will ask. You should also have been taking notes, or making mental ones, during the interview. The questions need to be about the job, your responsibilities and the kinds of projects on which you'd be working. Questions that focus on the company's needs and the opportunity. To get you started, there's a list of questions you can use (and ones to avoid) at the end of this chapter.

This is also a great time to bring up any particular skill, talent or accomplishment that the interviewer has not asked about. If you have won any awards or recognition at a previous position or while in school, now's your chance to mention it.

When you tell her about your special skill, talent or accomplishment, be sure to put it in context. Just telling her out of the blue that you were a resident adviser while you lived in the dorms at good ol' State U. is not enough. Relate that accomplishment to how and why you were selected for the position. Let her know how fierce the competition was and that they chose only 4 out of 120 applicants. Explain how this was a position of responsibility and importance. You weren't simply the person to whom residents turned when they were locked out of their rooms. You may have only a few moments to share something that you want to bring to the interview. Don't waste this precious opportunity on a story that does not advance your cause.

This is your chance to separate yourself from the pack. Think about what differentiates you from all the other candidates the interviewer might be seeing. Tell her something memorable, perhaps even something intriguing that makes her want to know more about you and makes you stick out in her mind later when she is trying to remember you after having seen scores of applicants. Just remember to keep the anecdote job or work related. If it is a story from outside of the workplace, perhaps a leadership position that you held with your religious or political group, make sure that she understands why you are using this story and take care not to mention which religious group or your political affiliation. Many interviewers get nervous when candidates bring up the topic of religion or politics. Reassure her that you are using this story only to make a work-related point, not to open up a conversation about your private beliefs. Newer entrants to the workforce or younger candidates just out of school may use a school-related example. Talking about a team you were on or a sport or activity in which you participated is a great way to demonstrate to the interviewer that you are a team player, someone who can put personal goals aside for the good of the group. This is a trait that is very highly valued, especially in lower-level positions in which you will often have to work as part of a team rather than as the team leader.

The sharing portion of the interview can be the most enjoyable. But this is also the time when many candidates slip. Don't get so relaxed that you forget why you're there. At this point in the interview, the interviewer may put down the pad on which she's been taking notes, lean back in her chair and relax a bit herself. Recognize that this may all be a ploy to get you to let down your guard as well. Stay vigilant and on message. Yes, she does want to hear about your special skills and accomplishments, but this is also a time when many candidates talk about things that ought not come up in the interview, such as your feelings about a difficult boss or problems you've had with co-workers. This part of the interview needs to be planned as carefully as the stories you use in your answers.

CLOSING

This is the part of the interview when the interviewer turns into a salesperson. Ideally, a good interviewer will use this time to make sure that you have had a good interview and, regardless of whether you are being considered for the position, that you leave their office thinking well of the company. Even if you're no longer a candidate (in their minds) you may still be a consumer. Or even better, for the recruiter, a pipeline to other candidates.

You may recognize that you have entered the closing portion of the interview from the interviewer's physical behavior. The interviewer may shift in her chair, rearrange the papers in front of her or close the pad on which she has been taking notes. Pay close attention to her body language. Your candidacy might, to some degree, be evaluated on your ability to pick up on nonverbal communication. This is a skill that is very often cited as one of the so-called intangibles that people use when making a hiring decision. When determining if there was a good chemistry between you and the interviewer, your sensitivity to unspoken cues can sink or advance your candidacy. Particularly if the interviewer knows that the manager she is recruiting for is one who doesn't say much but expects everyone who works for him to figure out what he wants. Your ability to pick up on nonverbal communication is not just a plus in your favor but could also be critical to your being considered for the next interview.

As the interview starts to wrap up, be careful not to allow any sense of desperation creep into your voice or demeanor. It's very easy at this point to think, "I blew it, she hates me, and she can't wait out get me out of her office." All interviews end. You need to prepare and have some scripted phrases in mind, in the same way that you had some great opening phrases you made sure to work in during the icebreaker portion of the interview. Your last impression is just as important, and in some ways more important, than your first impression.

Think about it. If your first impression had been bad and you hadn't done anything to change her mind, then you would have been out of her office long ago. But the fact that you have successfully made it through all or most of the interview counts for a lot. Knowing how to end the interview on a professional note and with a competent tone is critical to getting to the next step. If your candidacy is on the bubble, very often the way you handle the end of the interview will tip the decision in your favor.

This is the time to ask about next steps. Instead of just asking standard questions like, "When will I hear from you?" or "When do you expect to make a decision?" you need to frame the recruiter's answer. Otherwise your question is sure to get a standard answer.

"We have a number of candidates yet to see. However we hope to be able to make a decision sometime in the next couple of weeks." Sound familiar?

The other response you might get is, "Because of the volume of interest in this outstanding position, we will only be able to contact those candidates with whom we will be pursuing this fantastic opportunity." "Outstanding position," "fantastic opportunity." Remember, I told you that this is when the recruiter puts on the salesperson hat.

Don't be taken in by the interviewer's superlatives. This could also be her way of saying, "We aren't going to get back to you. In fact, we won't respond to the majority of the people who inquire about the job or who we interview." Unfortunately, this is a cold fact of the job market today. Between 80% and 90% of all resumes do not even get an automatically generated e-mail response. More than 50% of people who actually get interviewed, over the phone or in person, do not hear back from the company unless they pursue a response. You need to take steps in your closing to make sure that you are not one of the people to fall into this black hole of no responses. You also need to frame your follow-up call so you'll be better positioned to get past the gatekeeper.

One of the things that salespeople say is, "You have to ask for it." So, in this instance, when you ask about next steps, don't leave it vague or ambiguous. Instead of asking, "When should I follow-up about your decision?" use a closed-end question. "Should I follow up with you later this week or early next? Which day would be best?" When you give the interviewer a choice like this, she will almost always choose the later date, but at least when you call back you can bypass the gatekeeper by saying that you were instructed to call back on this day.

Some people advise candidates to put the interviewer on the spot. "So, how'd I do? Will you be referring me to the next round?" Most people don't like being put on the spot that way, and it is still too easy for the interviewer to say, "We really won't know until we've completed all the interviews and had the chance to review all the candidates." So this type of aggressive behavior won't necessarily get you what you want and it can very easily poison any good impression you've made up to that point.

Still, you want there to be some call to action at the end of the interview. Outline if you can what the next steps will be, such as if the interviewer will call you or if you will call her. Identify the best time and day to call and then be sure to call back when you say you will. Again, one of the intangibles that recruiters like to see is tenacity and perseverance. Make the follow-up calls and don't get discouraged. Even if you are the number one candidate, you are going to get voicemail sometimes. For tips on how to deal with voicemail stress, take a look at the chapter on what to do when recruiters don't return your calls. I know one recruiter who doesn't call a candidate back after an interview just to see how long it takes for the candidate to call him. Initiative is prized in his organization. He's looking for aggressive people who go after what they want or need. If you don't follow up with him after an interview, but wait for him to call you, well, let's just say that you're not going to be working at his firm.

At the end of the interview you need to let the recruiter know of your interest in the position and the company. If you aren't confident that this is the perfect position for you, or even close to perfect, you still want to leave the recruiter thinking well of you. Recruiters talk to one another. You want to be sure that you are leaving a completely positive impression. You want this recruiter to refer you to others within the company, or even outside, if she can't offer the job to you. If you have made a good impression on her, you are the person she will most likely refer to others when given the opportunity. This is just one reason that it is imperative not to get mad if you sense that this is not going to be your day.

Finally, while you may not be considered for this position, you don't know what the next opening at this company is going to be. You may be perfect for it and it might be perfect for you. If you show any frustration with the interview or react as if you feel that you're being rushed out of the room, you are not going to be called back the next time the interviewer has an opening, even if you have all the skills for that job. You will be eliminated on chemistry.

SUCCESS DOES NOT NECESSARILY MEAN TAKING THE JOB

I know that sounds ridiculous to you if you're unemployed, but success can mean accurately determining that this is the right job to accept and it can also mean knowing when to turn down an offer. Success can also mean knowing that you've done everything right to research and prepare for an interview. Sometimes the hiring decision comes down to something that has nothing to do with your qualifications. A few years back I had a friend who made it to the final cut for a job. They were going to hire her or someone else. The two candidates had virtually identical credentials. Either one could have done the job. The company went with the other candidate because they didn't like my friend's hairstyle. Hairstyle! This, in my opinion, is a sad reflection on the company's hiring practice; but it was completely beyond my friend's control. And for those of you wondering, hirsuteness—or lack thereof—is not a protected category.

THE GOAL OF THE INTERVIEW

Okay, I am somewhat biased in my approach to interviews. Having been a recruiter, I like interviews. When handled properly by a skilled recruiter and a prepared candidate, interviews seem like conversations between two people who are interested in the same thing. And that's essentially what they are. You are both interested in filling an open position with the best person. The only difference is that the recruiter does not yet realize that the best person is sitting right there in front of her. That's your goal for the interview, especially the first interview. Your ultimate goal is to get an offer and accept the job. But at the first interview your goal is to get to the next level: to make the interviewer see the benefit in hiring you. You do this by making sure the recruiter clearly sees your skills, talents and passion for the job. To accomplish all this you must carefully prepare for the interview long before you get into the room or on the phone with the recruiter.

To be ultimately successful when interviewing, remember the four **P**'s:

- **P**reparation is the key that opens the door,
- **P**ractice is the vehicle to guide you in the right direction,
- **P**assion turbo-charges your presentation, and
- **P**ersuasiveness will get you across the finish line.

INTERVIEW TIPS

Here's a quick summary to review before your next interview:

- **Plan to arrive at the interview at least 15 minutes before the scheduled time.** One thing that you can count on is that on the day of the interview, something will go wrong to delay you (coffee spills, missed train connection, weather).

    If the interview is in a place that you've never been to before, consider taking a trip to the interview site a day or two prior to the interview, if possible, to be sure that you know exactly where you're going.

- **Use the bathroom before your interview.** Yes, this sounds silly, but people forget. You'll be able to focus more on the interview if you're not squirming in your seat. This is one more reason to arrive 15 minutes early.

In winter, even if you don't need to use the bathroom, go there and wash your hands under hot water. No one likes to shake a really cold hand. It can give a subliminal bad first impression.

- **Dress appropriately for the organization.** This does not necessarily mean showing up in your navy blue interview suit. Learn as much as you can about the culture of the organization before you walk in the door so you look like you already work there.

  Consider removing any "facial hardware." Unless you're interviewing at some Internet start-up, err on the side of caution.

- **Walk in with confidence.** The person you're meeting with is not there to trip you up, sink you or make you look bad. You just might be the solution to their problem.

  Walk in assuming that you are what they're looking for. All the people in the department are overworked and waiting for someone who will pitch in and help carry the load. Don't be cocky, but walk in envisioning that you are this person.

- **Make eye contact.** Looking at the floor or the plants will not impress anyone.

  When responding to the interviewer's questions, always take a breath before answering. There are no awards for speed. It's better to compose your thoughts and be sure you're answering the question they asked. They won't remember how quickly you answered, but how well.

- **Answer slowly and carefully.** Be sure that you've heard the entire question correctly before you start answering.

  Do not interrupt the interviewer before he finishes asking the question because you think you know the answer. Listening skills are very much prized by organizations.

  If the interviewer seems distracted, wait until the focus is back on you. Don't start talking if the interviewer is not ready to listen.

If you're really stumped, you can tell the interviewer, "I really want to give you a good answer, so just give me a moment."

- **Recognize the different types of questions.** The two most common are: behavioral and hypothetical situations.

  Behavioral questions ask about specific examples of how you have handled real situations in the past.

  Hypothetical situation questions ask what you would do if you were in the job or in a specific situation. You can spot a hypothetical situation question when you hear the words "if" or "would."

- **At the end of the interview, establish what the next steps will be.** Instead of asking when they'll follow up or when you should follow up, give a choice. Use a closed-end question to narrow down the specific day when you should call back.

  When you call, say, "I'm calling you back as you requested," so it seems like it was his or her idea. This is also a good way to get past the "gatekeeper," the secretary or receptionist whose job it is to screen calls and keep people like you away from the decision maker. Simply say, " [Name of person] asked me to call today."

- **Ask when they hope or plan to fill this position.** This is a better way to ask about their timetable for making a decision than asking for a start date.

- **Ask for a business card** or contact information from every person with whom you meet.

- **Assume the best** and expect to have a good time in the interview.

- **Do your best to make it a conversation** rather than a ping-pong match.

AFTER THE INTERVIEW

- **Once you are out of the building, make notes** about what was discussed while the interview is fresh in your mind.

  Send a thank you note within 24 hours and follow up with a call within a week.

- **Do what you say you will do.** If you say that you will call back, call back, regardless of how you think the interview went.

  If you are asked to send some follow-up information, send it promptly, on the same day if possible, before they forget that they asked for it.

- **Keep a log of your interviews.** List the following:
  1. Whom you met.
  2. The names of any other people with whom you spoke.
  3. The name of the secretary, assistant and/or receptionist. This will come in handy when you are making your follow-up call.
  4. Any dates that were agreed to for follow up.
  5. The outcomes of all follow-up phone calls and e-mails.

ONE FINAL TIP

Keep your handkerchief, if you carry one (and you should) in your left back pocket, not your right. If you have to sneeze during an interview, you will use your left hand to pull out the handkerchief, not the hand you use to shake the interviewer's hand. Some women prefer to carry their handkerchief or tissues in their purse. That's fine but the same rule applies when using one. Use your left hand to cover your nose and mouth when you sneeze.

Even though I've made such a big deal about what to do if you sneeze, do not go into the interview worrying, "What if I sneeze?" You have enough on your mind and it is very unlikely that you will. If you forget and use your right hand, it's not the end of the world. Just reach for the Purell you also keep in your pocket or purse so that you can disinfect your hands before shaking hands with the interviewer at the end of the interview. You will impress them doubly with how prepared you are.

If you don't carry some kind of hand sanitizer with you, you will be faced with a choice at the end of the interview. You can either ask to use their Purell if you see it on the desk somewhere (you will be amazed at how many recruiters keep this right out in the open) or you can beg off from shaking their hand at the end of the interview on the basis that you do not want to give them any germs. Either way the recruiter will appreciate your thoughtfulness.

QUESTIONS TO USE IN THE SHARING PORTION OF THE INTERVIEW

- What kind of project teams might I get involved with?
- What are some of the greatest challenges facing the company today? Facing the department I'll be joining?
- What kind of feedback can I expect about my performance? How frequently is it given?
- What kind of training and development opportunities would I have? Would I have any input into my training and development plan with my manager?
- Will I have much interaction with staff outside my department?
- How do you see my skills complementing the department?
- Is there any training I'd need right off the bat to start contributing to the team's success?
- What parts of the organization does this department interact with most frequently?
- What do you expect the person you hire to contribute to the team (or department or organization) in the next 6 to 12 months?

The beauty of that last question is that while it is focused on the needs of the organization and your contribution, you can also find out what it is that the organization is looking for in filling this position. This will help you a great deal in framing your answers and additional questions for future interviews.

QUESTIONS OR TOPICS TO AVOID, ESPECIALLY IN A FIRST OR SCREENING INTERVIEW

I wish I could tell you I was making these up, but these are all questions that people have asked in first interviews. In most cases, they did not get a second interview.

- When will I start?
- What kind of benefits do you offer?
- How much vacation/sick days/personal days do I get? When can I take them?
- How soon will I get a salary/performance review?
- How soon will I be eligible for a promotion? To post for another position?
- Why is this position open? What happened to the last person?
- Is there on site child care?
- Will I be able to telecommute?
- Will I get to attend any conferences out-of-town?
- Will I have my own office?
- Can I bring my pet to work? Is there much travel?
- What's the starting salary?

If you must ask about salary, and at some point you will, it's better to ask for a range or to ask about the organization's compensation philosophy. Does the organization target starting salaries at the midpoint of the market? Are they above midpoint? Is it the kind of organization that starts below midpoint but offers accelerated salary reviews (i.e., every six months for the first three years) to bring you up to market. All of these are valid approaches to compensation and asking about their philosophy makes you look like a savvier candidate who has done his homework on the industry.

The main difference between the two preceding list of questions is that the first list is all about the job and the company and what you can do for them. The second list is all focused on you and what the company can do for you. Remember what John Kennedy said: "Ask not what your country can do for you; ask what you can do for your country."

Nine

PROBING QUESTIONS
What did she mean by that?

In the last chapter, we talked about the overall structure of the interview. This chapter deals specifically with the heart of any interview, the questions you will be asked.

There are four primary types of questions. I'll review each with several examples as well as strategies for answering them. To effectively answer any question, it is imperative that you recognize the type of question it is and are clear about what information you are being asked.

LEARN TO LISTEN, THEN LISTEN TO LEARN
All too often candidates jump in and start answering before being completely clear about what's being asked. One person whom I was counseling told me about a question he had been asked on an interview before we started working together. He'd been asked:

"Everyone knows that there is sometimes tension between departments in an organization. Tell me about a time when you had to communicate some bad news about a deadline that was not going to be met. How did you go about it? How did you resolve the situation?"

He launched into a comprehensive response about his communication skills. The candidate explained about taking responsibility and going directly to the manager of the other department, face-to-face and man-to-man. He explained how he forthrightly and directly explained that his department was not going to be able to get a shipment out to a client by the date that had been committed to. After the candidate finished very proudly explaining the depth of his communication skills, the interviewer had only one follow-up question.

"But what did you do about satisfying the client?"

The interviewer, in a very canny fashion, had tested the candidate's listening skills. And this candidate didn't get the job.

What the interviewer really wanted to know about was the candidate's problem-solving skills. This man misread the question. The interviewer was interested in more than how he had communicated the problem. The interviewer wanted to know what the candidate had done to resolve the situation of meeting the commitment to the client. His organization had a reputation for customer satisfaction. The interviewer wanted to know how the problem had been resolved and if the candidate had shown creativity and initiative in addressing the situation. This was not a communication skills question. The candidate had not done a thorough enough job of learning everything he could about the organization. If he had, he might have answered differently.

It's easy to make a mistake when answering. It is important to listen carefully to the entire question and identify which type of question it is, so that you are best prepared to give the kind of response the interviewer seeks.

BROAD-BASED QUESTIONS

Broad-based questions are often used early in an interview. These may seem easier to answer and are often used as a transition from the introduction or icebreaker phase of the interview into the probing phase. Broad-based questions may appear easier to answer but require the same attention and care as any other question. Sample broad-based questions include:

- Could you tell me about a typical day at your current (or last) job?
- What are some of your current responsibilities?
- Why are you interested in this position with this company?
- What do you enjoy most about your current position? (Be aware that very often this is only a set-up question for the next question ...)
- What do you like least? (Inexperienced interviewers often telegraph their questions.)
- How do you feel that you achieve your greatest success—working alone or as part of a team? (Don't assume that being a "team player" is the right answer. The organization may be looking for someone who can work alone and has a lot of initiative. Do your homework as to the values of this organization.)

Notice that in all of these instances you will have the opportunity to explain a lot about how you like to work, what gets you excited about doing this kind of work or why you want to work for this company. This type of question allows you a lot of latitude in how you answer, but keep your answers job related. Keep the focus on why it would be good for the company to hire you, not why it would be good for you to get hired. Use your answers to expand on your broad or specific skill set. Talk about your goals and your desires and how these align with the objectives of the organization. Tell the interviewer why hiring you will be beneficial for the department and how you expect to fit in and support your co-workers.

Whenever possible use your answers to give examples of how and when you have done good work. Explain how your past accomplishments demonstrate your proven ability to get the job done. This is no time for one-word answers. Look for opportunities to make the viability of your candidacy clear.

HYPOTHETICAL WORK SITUATIONS

Hypothetical work situations are great opportunities to demonstrate your creativity to the interviewer. In these questions, recognizable from the presence of the words *if* and *would*, you will be presented with a potential work situation and asked how you would respond if this happened to you on the job. This is a time when you may be tempted to try to think of the "right" answer, but it is more important to answer honestly, remaining truthful to how you would really respond. An experienced interviewer will be able to tell if you are giving a politically correct or sanitized response instead of your actual feelings.

Hypothetical work situations are used to determine your judgment and your creativity. You will often be presented with a situation that seems like a choice between the fire and the frying pan. When presented with two options that seem equally bad, the interviewer may want to see if you can come up with a third, more palatable solution. Or it might be his way of testing to see how you weigh the two alternatives to come to a decision. This is why you shouldn't spend a lot of time trying to figure out the right answer. Even if you do come up with what might be the better of the two choices in the interviewer's mind, he may challenge your answer just to see how you defend it. He may want to see how well you have thought out your decision.

In the workplace we are often called upon to defend our decisions. The recruiter may know that the manager you'll be working for likes to play devil's advocate. He doesn't necessarily dislike your ideas, but he tries to poke holes in them to explore their viability. This can be very unnerving to some people. If the recruiter knows this is the person that you'll be reporting to, then he needs to test how well you'll stand up under that kind of scrutiny. This is a chance for him to determine not just if you're smart enough for the job but if you have the personality that will allow you to remain productive under this kind of interrogation. When subjected to cross-examination, some people tend to fold and go along with whatever the manager wants. This may not be best for the organization. The recruiter may be aware of the kind of employee who has flourished in this environment and the kind who has bolted within the first three months. He needs to find out which kind of employee you'd be.

Examples of hypothetical work situations include:

- If you were working on an important project and a manager from another department came and asked for your help on her project, what would you do?
- How would you determine how to use your time if you had two projects with concurrent deadlines?
- What would you do if you were working on a very important project for your boss and his boss came and insisted that you drop whatever you were doing to work on something that you thought was not as critical?
- If you saw a co-worker doing something minor that you thought might be against policy, would you tell the person to stop or would you tell your supervisor? What if you told them to stop and they told you to "Mind your own business"?
- What would you do if a long tenured co-worker asked you to slow down the speed of your work so as to not make the others look bad?
- What would you do if you were blamed for something that you had nothing to do with?

These aren't easy questions. In many instances you might think that there is no right answer. That's why it's important to respond as honestly as possible to what you would actually do on the job. The interviewer is not trying to trick you. He is trying to evaluate your candidacy. The only way he can do this is if you give him the best information about how you'd really react to a situation.

Another benefit to answering honestly is that it allows you to evaluate the company to determine if the culture of the organization is consistent with your moral compass. What if, in response to the question about the co-worker who was breaking the rules, you say that you'd report it to your supervisor? If the recruiter questions this response saying that minor infractions of policy are okay if it's in the name of increasing productivity, you have to think about if you want to work for a place that is lax about the rules. If hired, how would you know which policies must be obeyed to the letter of the law and which are bendable? This can create a lot of tension for you once you are on the job. Work is stressful enough without worrying about the unwritten rules that actually govern the place. You have to determine if this culture is consistent with an environment in which you can do your best work.

Hypothetical work situation questions are also a great opportunity for you to demonstrate your creativity. Your answers to hypothetical questions, by their very nature, must also be hypothetical. So this is an opportunity to let your imagination run wild, within the parameters of answering realistically. This is not time to be constrained by the nagging doubts in the back of your head. You'd like to say exactly what you'd do in the hypothetical situation but think, "They'd never go for that." How do you know? This is your chance to impress the interviewer with your creativity, by thinking out of the box as everyone tells you to do. Go for it! The interviewer has already probably heard many safe answers, and this is not time to play it safe. Go for broke. It's hypothetical and this is your chance to have some fun.

If you're really worried that your answer is too off the wall, you can preface your response by saying something to the effect of, "I'm not sure if this is exactly how your policy manual says to handle this, but here's one thing I could do in this situation…" and then it's off to the races. This is the part of the interview in which your creativity and judgment are being explored, and creativity and judgment are not mutually exclusive. You can be creative and show good judgment, and this is your chance to do just that.

COMPARISON QUESTIONS

Comparison questions, also known as "compare and contrast questions," can be some of the most difficult questions to answer, but these also give you the greatest chance to show off the depth of your knowledge on a topic. Comparison questions are a staple of technical interviews. When I say technical I'm not just talking about computers. Comparison questions are a great way to explore the depth of your understanding about the technical aspects of any position. There are technical elements to selling, marketing, human resources, and teaching. These are the tactical skills requisite for success in the position.

Salespeople might be asked to explain the difference between a direct and indirect approach to selling, and when to use each kind. A nurse manager whom I was coaching came up with "Tell me the different ways to start an IV and when you'd use each." These are a style of comparison question that is known as "which do you prefer and why". Again, a big part of your answer is the ability to defend your choice. However, in a comparison question, as opposed to a hypothetical work situation, there very often is a right answer. Comparison questions used to test your knowledge or technical skills require that you know what you're talking about.

Another variety of comparison question may be used to determine why you are interested in working for this organization. This is one of my favorite questions and it is important to recognize it for the trap it can be.

- Compare your current (or most recent) position to the position that you've applied for with our company. How are they the same and how are they different?"

What your interviewer may be trying to figure out here is what's your motivation for wanting this job. Be very careful in answering this question. If you say that you're trying to get away from the constant pressure and deadlines at your current position and are looking for a place that has a better work/life balance, you will have eliminated yourself from consideration if the interviewer knows that the department you'd be joining is always staring at a deadline or quota. Should you wax poetic about the opportunity to innovate new ideas and the freedom to try to discover original applications, you're out of the running if the organization is looking for someone to strictly follow protocols. Don't think that I'm suggesting you always play it safe when answering this type of question. It's important to recognize that what the interviewer is really trying to do when asking this question is gauge if your perception of the organization has anything to do with how the place really operates. If you have an unrealistic view of your potential new company, the interviewer is apt to keep looking.

Since so many compare and contrast questions are specific to the technical aspects of a position, it's hard to give examples of specific ones you'll hear, but you can generally recognize them by the "either/or" structure they take.

- A programmer may be asked, "What's the difference between C++ and Java and when would you use one as opposed to the other?"
- A broker might be asked the different strategies to use in a bull market versus a slower-growth period.
- A salesperson may be asked the different ways to sell to older as opposed to younger buyers.

Notice in each case the candidate is being asked to compare one technique or knowledge to another. This is the hallmark of compare and contrast questions.

BEHAVIOR-BASED QUESTIONS

The most common form of interview questions in use today is behavior-based. Most interviewers are taught at some point in their career that past performance is the best predictor of future performance. So interviewers dig like terriers to find out exactly how you've behaved on the job. Using behavior-based questions is the best way to explore your work ethic and effectiveness.

Behavior-based questions are similar to hypothetical work situations in that you will be presented with a real work situation but instead of being asked how you *would* respond *if* you were in that situation, you will be asked how you *did* respond when faced with this situation in the past. Your first thought might be, "what if I've never faced that situation in the past?" Relax. These questions are usually based on the kind of situations that anyone who has been in the kind of position for which you are applying has seen. So you will not be asked any behavior-based questions about lion taming when you apply for a job as a programmer.

A behavior-based question often starts with the phrase "Tell me about a time..." or "Give me an example..." The interviewer wants a real example of how you've behaved when faced with this before. So now is the time to pull out your anecdotes, war stories and accomplishments. Tell her about the time you saved the company $4 million. Tell her how your solution reduced processing time and expense by 27%. Just be sure to correlate the accomplishment you describe to the business of the organization to which you're applying. If you've gotten some sense of the culture of the organization, take this opportunity to relate your work ethic to the values of the firm. Tell a story about being part of a successful task force if teamwork is what's valued. Describe how you stayed until 11:00 PM four nights running if persistence and doing whatever it takes is the company's expected behavior when dealing with a crisis.

Behavior-based questions often have two or three parts and so will your answer. Some interviewers will ask the entire question and then sit back to hear your answer. Others will go for a more conversational style and ask one piece of the question at a time. The difference sounds like this:

"Tell me about a time that you had to resolve a dispute between two co-workers when there was no supervisor around. How did you approach the situation and what were the results of your efforts?"

The more conversational approach will allow you to answer each part of the question before proceeding to the next.

Q: "Tell me about a time that you had to resolve a dispute between two co-workers when there was no supervisor around."

A: "I once had to get in between two guys on the loading dock when we were putting in a lot of OT during the holiday rush. We were so busy and the supervisor couldn't be everywhere and these two guys couldn't agree on the order to load things onto the truck."

Q: "What did you do in that situation? It must've been a little scary and you had no authority to step in, did you?"

A: "No, but they looked like they were about to start fighting. We were all pretty stressed out because we'd all been putting in lots of OT and the holidays were right around the corner. The first thing I did was get a couple of the other guys to get in between them and stop them from yelling at each other and chest bumping.

Q: "Was that effective? Did you resolve their conflict?"

A: "First I had to separate them, then I spoke with each of them and then the three of us worked it out together. Finally we were able to get back to work."

In the second example, the interviewer got to the same place, but did it in a more conversational manner. A good interviewer will adapt his or her style to the candidate to get the best information. Your job as the candidate is to recognize the style of questioning and go with the flow of the interview. Don't try to say too much at first until you feel confident that you and the interviewer are in a rhythm. As in any good conversation the goal is to create a dialogue.

BE THE STAR OF YOUR INTERVIEW

Another way to be sure to answer behavior-based questions effectively is to remember the acronym STAR. This stands for Situation, Task, Action and Result. Some recruiters use the acronym SOAR, substituting the word "Objective" for "Task." For some more senior or strategic positions, it might be more appropriate to focus on the objective rather than the task, but the point is the same. Break down your answer into the four component parts when responding to a question.

114

What is the situation that you were faced with, what task or objective did you have to complete as part of the project, what action did you take to effectively and correctly complete the task and, what was the result of your action. Using this acronym will help you to remember to thoroughly answer any behavior-based question. Here's a roadmap for breaking down the story of one of your successes.

- Think about one of your accomplishments at work. Perhaps a task force or project team on which you served. Now why was that task force assembled? What was the objective of getting all these people together? What problem were you supposed to tackle?
- Define what role you served on the task force and describe the tasks assigned to you or that you volunteered for. How did you approach your role?
- Answer as specifically as possible in outlining your contribution to the project and the actions you took.
- Finally, summarize your answer in explaining the results of the actions you took. Whenever possible quantify your results in hard numbers, dollars and cents or percentage improved.

An example might sound like this: "Absenteeism was running extremely high in one department. I was asked to serve on a task force to investigate the problem, make some recommendations as to how to lower absenteeism and implement the best of the suggestions. We considered a lot of ideas to encourage people to come to work more reliably and my idea was to create a perfect-attendance program. It was simple, easy to administer and it rewarded people for doing what we wanted them to do —show up regularly. I researched other organizations that had similar programs and designed a program that worked for this particular unit. We rolled out the program and it was so successful that after the first year we extended the program to other departments. After three years we had reduced absenteeism by almost 20%, which resulted in a cost savings of over $700,000."

In its component parts this answer reads as follows:

- **Situation:** Absenteeism was running extremely high in one department.
- **Task:** I was asked to serve on a task force to investigate the problem, make some recommendations as to how to lower absenteeism and implement the best of the suggestions.
- **Action:** We batted around a lot of ideas to encourage people to come to work more reliably and my idea was to create a perfect-attendance program. It was simple, easy to administer and it rewarded people for doing what we wanted them to do—show up regularly. I researched other organizations that had similar programs and designed a program that worked for this particular unit.
- **Result:** We rolled out the program and it was so successful that after the first year we extended the program to other departments. After three years we had reduced absenteeism by almost 20%, which resulted in a cost savings of over $700,000.

This is an effective and structured way to answer a behavior-based question. It is also very important to note that even though the candidate was replying about a project team on which he had served, he was careful to detail his specific contributions to the eventual outcome.

This brings up two delicate subjects in interviews. First, when you are talking about your accomplishments relative to a task force or project team, you have to say "we" a lot and this is a red flag to many interviewers. Expect that you will be probed a lot about your specific role and contributions to the project. So short-circuit the interviewer's questions by volunteering this information. Be clear about what the team accomplished and how your service to the team made that happen. The second question is how much credit to take for the team's success. It may be tempting to overstate your contribution. I mean, how are they going to know exactly how much you did or didn't do? They'll never be able to verify this one story. So what's the harm in exaggerating a little?

Simply put: never lie in an interview. It will come back to haunt you. Mark Twain once said, "Always tell the truth, that way you don't have to remember what you said." This advice from a man who was renowned for telling tall tales! But he was right. In the next chapter we'll address how you talk about times when you weren't as successful at work as you wish you'd have been, and how to turn that talk to your advantage.

BRAINTEASER QUESTIONS

Abstract, or brainteaser, questions are daunting to some people and a day at the beach for others. Some candidates love the challenge of an off-the-wall question. This is the fun part of the interview. They get to stop talking about the job so much and go off on flights of fancy. For many, this is when the interview gets really conversational and less like a tennis match. Others have no idea of how to answer when asked, "If you are standing on the bank of the Mississippi River, how much water passes the point where you're standing in one hour?" The key to answering a brainteaser well is to recognize it for what it is and what it is not. First, relax; they do not expect you to have the answer to this question. What the interviewer is doing is probing you to see how you would come up with an answer to the question. A correct answer to the question above starts with damming the mighty Mississippi, something that is not likely to happen. But this type of question is designed to further probe your creativity and how you think. It is well known that problem solving is a much sought after and valued quality in applicants. Brainteasers are one way to see just how far outside the box you are capable of and willing to think.

Not all companies use brainteasers in their interviews. Many high-tech companies do, and many use them incorrectly. Interviewers who use brainteasers should be trained in how to evaluate the responses. Unfortunately, this is not always the case. Lots of interviewers use brainteasers simply because they are new, trendy, or perhaps they've heard that their competition is using them.

There is no way to determine a right answer to most brainteaser questions. An interviewer who uses brainteasers effectively will ask you these impossible questions with a perfectly straight face. He wants you to take the question seriously and answer it to the best of your ability. Your initial response may be to blurt out, "There's no way to answer that question" or "Are you serious?" This may not be the best tack to take. Yes, he is serious. And if you point out the absurdity of the question you may be demonstrating that you are not the best-qualified candidate that he will see today. Some people will play along with this line of questioning. But this is not play; this is a very serious part of the interview because this is the interviewer's chance to see how you tackle a problem that can't actually be solved. Are you defeated by the impossible nature of the question? Do you rise to the challenge and actually get excited at the prospect of even attempting to answer this question?

People who do not care for this particular line of questioning but recognize the need to answer may want to frame the question within their own reality. In answering this question they will start by acknowledging that the solution will not work but here's what they would do if the impossible were possible.

"Okay, recognizing that it is not possible to dam up the Mississippi and carefully set up a system for measuring how much water passes through a measured opening, it's pretty near impossible to answer this question. But if I could do that, here is what I'd do..." and then off you go. It's okay to get the abstract nature of the question out in the open before answering. This also buys you a little time to come up with an appropriate answer.

Some candidates will apply a scientific approach to a question like this. Analyzing the width and depth of the river, measuring the speed at which the water is moving, and calculating the effect of barometric pressure on water currents, how close you are to the delta and the impact of motorized river traffic at the time of day that you are being asked to measure. Unfortunately, this is not likely the type of answer that the interviewer is looking for. If you insist on answering this way, you will likely be asked an even more abstract question that cannot be answered in weights, measures or knots. So while it is okay to answer like this, because you have to be true to your own style, this may not put you at the head of the candidate list. But that's okay too, because if the style and culture of the organization is to use questions such as these, it may not be the most compatible organization for someone who prefers to work in a different way.

Brainteasers sometimes take a while to explain because you have to be presented with the problem to be solved. Stay with the interviewer as he explains this all and listen for clues to determine what skill or style of behavior the interviewer is probing for. It's not always creativity or problem solving, but those are most often the traits for which the interviewer is looking.

Other examples of brainteasers that have been used are:

- Why are manhole covers round? If you've ever dropped a coin on a counter and seen the way it spins around until flat you can figure out the answer to this one.
- You are standing in an airplane hangar with a Boeing 747 that has to take off in two hours. There is not a scale in the world large enough to fit a 747. How much does it weigh? Saying that you will take the aircraft apart and weigh each component won't work because the plane has to take off in two hours. Saying that you will look up the weight in the manual in the cockpit or on the Internet is not the answer they are looking for either.
- A king has twin sons and can't decide which one to leave his throne to. He sends them off on a race, telling them that the prince whose horse comes in second will be next in line to the throne. The sons ride around for a few hours trying very carefully to stay behind the other. Finally, they come across a wise man who asks why the two princes are meandering

around in the forest. The princes dismount and explain the puzzle to the wise man. He says something to them and they both remount and ride as fast as they can back to the palace. What did the wise man tell the princes?

If you can't figure out the answers to these questions, or think you have and want to be sure, you can find the answers at www.SGGH.net. In the meantime, remember that there are no absolute right answers to these brainteasers but there are better ways to respond to impress the interviewer. The research you've done into the values of the organization will insure that your answers are among the better ones.

Successfully answering broad-based, hypothetical, comparison, behavior-based, and possibly brainteaser questions will extend the viability of your candidacy. You want to convince the interviewer, and ultimately the hiring manager, that you are the right person for the job. Carefully listening to the questions and thoughtfully responding is how you will do this.

Ten

ANSWERING TOUGH QUESTIONS

"Why did you leave your last job?"
and other fun interview questions

At some point during the interview you are going to be asked a question you wished the interviewer hadn't asked. In other words, they're going to ask you about a time when, to put it bluntly, you screwed up. You may be tempted to fabricate, stretch the truth or, put more simply, lie.

Don't.

When you get asked the so-called tough questions, you are being presented with an opportunity. We learn more from our mistakes than from our successes. This is an opportunity to talk about what you've learned from your mistakes. One of the most prized qualities in an employee is the ability to overcome adversity. This is your chance to describe how you remained focused when things weren't working out right. Use this question to describe what you'll do differently next time. Tell how you fixed the mistake. Dazzle your interviewer with your creativity, your resilience, your prowess in turning a potential failure into a rousing success. Or at least how you salvaged the situation.

WHAT HAVE YOU LEARNED?

I'm not just talking about putting a positive spin on a story. Take a long hard look at your failures. What did you learn from them? Which mistakes won't you make again? There are some failures that couldn't have been avoided. So be it. But was there something you could have done earlier in the course of events to prevent the situation from crashing and burning the way it did? There is always something else you could have done. If you are being honest with yourself you will find it.

One person I worked with said, "If I hadn't taken this crazy job five years ago, I never would have found myself in this situation." That may be going back a little too far, but how about this: When did you first realize that you worked in a crazy place or for a contender for the "Worst Boss" list? Why did you stay? What did you think you could accomplish? What steps did you take to improve the situation? Did it work? What else did you try? Be careful not to pin it all on the crazy boss. It's important that you don't come off as someone who points the finger of blame at someone else or who badmouths the boss. When you are formulating a positive story about a negative situation, you're going to have to work harder to find the way to have a positive light shine down on you. If you look hard enough, you can always find something positive to say about the experience. You can also use this as an opportunity to explain why you are currently unemployed and/or looking for a different job.

SHOULD I STAY OR SHOULD I GO?

Probably the most dreaded and for some the most difficult question to answer is, "Why did you leave your last job?" For this reason many will tell you to stay in a job, any job, even one you hate, just so you don't have to explain why you're not working. I agree that if you are thoroughly uncomfortable trying to answer this question or if it has tripped you up before, then yes, staying in any job is your best approach. On the other hand, if that job is sapping the life out of you, that will come through when you interview. Your desperation, frustration and exhaustion will creep into your presentation without your realizing it. The way you feel about your current job colors how you approach your next.

If you find yourself becoming bitter about work in general, then you need to think very carefully about how your current job is affecting you as you meet with potential employers. Do you appear desperate to get out of your current situation? Do you come across as angry? Would you consider taking a position as doorman to the seventh circle of Hell just to get away from your boss? Has your current job beaten down your enthusiasm so you don't appear as the vital, capable employee you know you can be? These are all the dangers of staying in a job you hate.

I was once working in a windowless file room. I was on a high floor, but my workspace was buried so deep in the core of the building that I had to walk out through three other workspaces just to see if it was raining outside. The building was equipped with the ubiquitous fluorescent light fixtures, there was no other source of natural light in my area, and the tubes over my desk were starting to go. Anyone who has ever dealt with this situation knows that the flickering of a dying fluorescent tube can drive you mad. In my case it was giving me blazing headaches searing across my skull. After a month of begging for the situation to be addressed, to no avail, I left that job. Fortunately, this was at a time when I could afford to be so cavalier, but I was dreading going into work every day. By 10:30 AM my temples were throbbing and once I got back to my desk after lunch I spent the afternoon with one eye on the clock. On the one hand, I was not being as productive as I could have been and needed to be, and on the other, I was in no shape to interview for another job as long as I was going to this one. This was an extreme situation in which getting out and having to answer the question was preferable to staying on the job to avoid having to explain my state of unemployment.

The final payoff was when I explained on interviews why I had left my last job. Everyone with whom I met understood, sympathized and said that they might have done the same thing. I used this as an opportunity to make myself out to be a dedicated employee who cared about doing an honest day's work as opposed to letting someone label me as a wimp or a quitter. You can make virtually any situation work to your advantage. You just need to figure out how.

One time, at an interviewing workshop that I was leading, there was a woman named Ellen handing out her business cards and resumes as fast as she could meet the other participants. No one at the session left without talking with her. I thought she was one of the best networkers I had ever seen, but I also sensed some desperation. When we finally had a chance to talk near the end of the first day, I got the whole story. She had only been at her company for about six weeks. She had interviewed and been hired to be a trainer. Before her start date, there had been a major restructuring at the company. The head of recruiting was fired and half the recruiting staff went with her. The head of Learning & Development, to whom Ellen was to report, now had the additional responsibility for recruiting until the firm could hire a new Director of Staffing. On Ellen's first day she was informed by her boss of the following: the organization was suddenly extremely short on recruiters; since Ellen was new to the company and hadn't yet mastered any of the training programs she'd expected to lead, she would switch over to be a recruiter instead of a trainer; and finally, since her boss was now covering two departments, she would have very little time if any to spend with Ellen. When Ellen pointed out that she had been hired as a trainer and had practically no experience as a recruiter, she was told to find a class on how to interview and take it. In the meantime, here's a bunch of open requisitions, now get to work on filling them.

Is it any wonder she was networking like crazy? It's hard to imagine anyone more motivated than Ellen to find another position. How will Ellen answer the question so many people dread in an interview? "Why did you leave your last position?" It is certainly less than prudent to say that your last boss was a lying double-crossing moron who wouldn't know how to manage if her life depended on it. Never badmouth a former manager in an interview. It was incumbent upon Ellen to find a way to explain what had happened at her soon-to-be former employer without sounding bitter, frustrated or vengeful. How would you tell her story if it had happened to you? It's not a bad idea to take a few horrible situations and practice writing up how you would have dealt with them. This will help you put your real life horror stories into perspective.

In this case, Ellen needed to shift the focus off her employer and on to her skills as a trainer. She didn't need to dwell on why she was looking. "There was a reorganization between the offer and my start date." She could just leave it at that and allow the interviewer to infer the rest. If pressed further, Ellen could go into some detail about having to take on a recruiter role, without mentioning that she wasn't suited for it and didn't want it. But she then needs to bring the conversation back to her talents and abilities as a trainer. If need be, Ellen can talk about pitching in and being the best recruiter she could be under the circumstances. Then explain that now she wants to get back to what she's truly passionate about, training managers and staff to do their jobs to the best of their ability, improve the productivity of the department, and positively impact the company's bottom line. All to redirect the interview toward how hiring Ellen benefits the company.

You don't have the emotional baggage that Ellen had in this situation. She was angry, felt betrayed, and was not at all happy about being out there looking for a job again. And yet there she was.

TOUGH QUESTIONS

You need to know what you are going to say in response to the tough questions.

- Were you fired or did you quit?
- Why couldn't you get along with your last boss?
- Why weren't you able to complete the assignment on time?

- Why did the project fail?
- Have there been other times when you had difficulty meeting your objectives?
- Can you think of any circumstances when you were better able to collaborate with others?
- What would you have changed about your last job?
- What could have convinced you to stay?

Recognize that these are all trap questions. In every instance, the interviewer is trying to corner you as having come up short in achieving the goal or objective. Each of these questions casts you and your candidacy in a negative light. How you present your story is how you will escape the negative taint.

The first key is not to accept the interviewer's portrayal. Politicians have been known to "frame" the debate. You need to do something similar. It is important to prepare how you will present those instances from your career when you may not have come out smelling like a rose. Face it, nobody's perfect. If you're worried that the interviewer is going to find out something in your work history that you'd rather not talk about, beat them to the punch. Tell them the story as you'd like it told. Frame the situation as a learning experience and explain what you've gotten from having been through this situation. What will you do differently the next time you're faced with this problem?

I can't script your answers for you, but think of it something like this:

Were you fired or did you quit?

"I *left* because there was a clear difference…" Do not accept either the word "fired" or "quit." Nobody brags about being fired, and even if the decision was yours, the word "quit" rarely has a positive connotation. Use this as an opportunity to explain how you analyze a situation and demonstrate your solid decision making skills. In this way you can set the parameters for the rest of the conversation. Leaving a bad job is a good thing and to your credit.

Why didn't you get along with your last boss?

"The way I approached the work and got things done didn't always mesh with my manager's style." Turn this negative into a positive by using this as a chance to make it clear that you got the work done. Do not make it a conversation about your ex-boss and his style. Your ex-boss is not applying for the job, you are. Steer the conversation to your accomplishments. As stated earlier, never badmouth anyone in an interview. It will lead the interviewer to wonder what you'll say about them if and when you are making your next move. Further, blaming the boss or your co-workers makes you sound like a complainer who does not take responsibility for your actions or situation. This is not the image you want to project.

Why weren't you able to complete the assignment on time?

Whenever a deadline is missed, there is usually some business reason for this. It is rarely solely because of the incompetence or negligence of one worker. Focus on this rather than your own shortcomings. It might have been the changing priorities of management, organizational restructuring or headcount and manpower shifts. Any and all of these contribute to deadlines being missed. Explain what happened in as neutral a way as possible.

Why did the project fail?

If the interviewer comes right out and calls the project a failure, then that's what it was in her eyes. You're not likely going to change her opinion so go for the next best thing. Be straightforward, accept accountability and make your willingness to take responsibility your strong strategic asset in this response. If you were the project manager and the project was not implemented successfully, then to many people, it has failed. Acknowledge that this was the case and impress her with your courage, then as quickly as possible segue over to what you learned from this failure. Failure is not a dirty word. If you never fail then you never know how much you can achieve.

When he was manager of the New York Yankees, Billy Martin had a simple rule for his base runners during spring training. If you didn't get picked off a base at least once during spring training, you got fined. He wanted every one of his ballplayers to know just how far a lead they could get off a base and still get back safely. The only way to accomplish this was to get picked off. Then you knew just how far was the edge of your ability. Players who never got picked off were not rewarded for their caution, and sometimes didn't even make the team.

Instead of focusing on failure, use this question as an opportunity to demonstrate your flexibility, your adaptability and your ability to overcome adversity. Explaining why the project didn't succeed is also an opportunity to describe your risk analysis techniques. How did you make the decisions you made? How did you choose to delegate, and to whom? How did you respond when you realized you weren't going to complete the project successfully? What steps did you take to try to salvage the project? Instead of talking about why a project failed, talk about all the myriad processes that went into your management of the process, whether you were managing others or working alone. Describe all the strategic elements that went into your decision-making. And again, don't forget to include what you've learned from this experience.

Have there been other times when you had difficulty meeting your objectives?

"Not really. In fact I usually complete my work and meet the objectives that my manager and I agreed upon." This question was the interviewer closing his mind to your candidacy. He's phrasing the question in such a way that he's trying to force you to talk about other projects that didn't work out as well as you had planned. What the interviewer is saying is that their opinion of you is that you are a person who has difficulty meeting objectives. You need to combat this by telling them clearly and concisely of times when you were successful and completed the objectives of the project. You need to change his mind before he closes the book. Use concrete examples of your behaviors and results. Remember to use the STAR (Situation, Task, Action, Result) or SOAR (Situation, Objective, Action, Result) technique to combat a question like this. The successful result is most important. Recognize that when you hear a question or comment like this, it's often the interviewer seeking information that confirms his first impression regardless of whether that first impression is accurate.

Can you think of any circumstances when you were better able to collaborate with others?

Give clear examples of when you successfully participated in a team effort. This sounds as if the interviewer is looking for a positive but watch out for the negative phrasing in the question. "Can you think of *any*..." What is left unsaid is that the interviewer so far has gotten the impression that you are not a team player. You are being given one last chance to prove that you can function as a member of the team. Whatever trait is being called into question, whether it is teamwork, initiative, creativity or flexibility, look for opportunities to give examples of your virtues, not your vices.

What would you have changed about your last job?

This is not an invitation for you to bash your last assignment. This question is actually probing your creativity. The interviewer is attempting to see if you just ran from a bad situation or if you did everything in your power to salvage it. This question is a wonderful opportunity to shine but keep your response within the guidelines of feasibility. No chocolate milk in the water fountains. Answer thoughtfully. You also want to make it clear that you are not simply abandoning a bad situation without having tried to make the best of it. If you did make suggestions about improving the workflow, then turn this hypothetical question into a behavioral one. Talk about all the things you did or tried to do to make your previous or current employer a more productive place.

There is one other thing to be on the lookout for when responding to this question. The interviewer could be using this question to find out what you don't like to do to compare it to the responsibilities of the position. Be sure to keep a positive spin on your answer when describing the improvements you would have implemented if you had been in charge.

What could have convinced you to stay?

There are a couple of uses for this question, from the interviewer's point of view. First, he may be gauging your commitment to the new job. Keep a forward focus when responding to this question. If you get all wistful about the position you are leaving (or have left) this could create some doubt in the interviewer's mind. Keep your answer very businesslike and brief. If you are interviewing while still employed, he may be checking to see if you are simply trying to get an offer letter to use as leverage to get a better raise from your current employer. It is better to respond by reiterating what interests you about the position that you are meeting to discuss. You are not meeting with this person to wax nostalgic about your old job, you are there to discuss and secure this new position. Keep your responses focused on the opportunity in front of you, not behind.

TOUGH SITUATIONS

There are other types of difficult questions that you'll be asked in interviews, not all of them legal. How you respond to these questions can have as much impact on your candidacy as your skills. These include questions about:

- Starting salary
- Gaps in your resume
- Having too much experience (a poorly camouflaged question about how old you are)
- Having no experience (for career shifters)
- Age, marital status, gender or child care (all of which are

illegal for the organization to use as the basis for hiring)
- Questions about your "assertiveness"

SO, HOW MUCH DO YOU WANT?

Salary—Try to defer any questions about compensation. You do not want to bring up salary too early and certainly not in a phone screen. It is not uncommon for someone who is screening via a telephone interview to ask about your salary requirements early in the phone call. If forced to give some kind of answer, give a range of salaries rather than one hard figure. The odds of your hitting the exact number that the organization has in mind for this opening are miniscule. Ideally you want the organization to make the first offer anyway. And they want to hear at what price you value your contribution. You can use phrases like, "I'm more interested in the contribution I'll make than the salary." But those will come off as pat deflections. Often it will only prompt the interviewer to pursue a hard figure that much more relentlessly. You can try saying that you "expect the salary will be market competitive for a person who brings as much to the position as I do" but this still may not suffice.

The best way to prepare for the inevitable salary question is to do your homework before you even apply. Do your best to know what "market value" is for your position and in your location. The same job will be priced differently in Los Angeles than in Lansing. Try to find out what the organization's compensation philosophy is. Are they a 90th percentile payer or are they known for starting low and accelerating once you prove your worth? All this information will help you to price yourself appropriately for this job. This is especially important when you are applying for positions outside of your local market. Candidates in large urban markets often overprice themselves when talking with interviewers from outside their area. Bottom line, the longer you can postpone this part of the process the longer you have to impress the interviewer.

WHAT WERE YOU DOING DURING THIS PERIOD?

Gaps—There will inevitably be gaps in your resume. Be sure that you can talk about something work related that you were doing during each of these gaps. Did you go back to school? Did you volunteer? Perhaps you assumed a leadership position in a charity or community group with which you are involved. All of these are valid uses of your time.

In today's environment a gap of several months is no longer the stigma it was a decade ago. Senior level positions can often take six to nine months to secure.

Raising your children is also a valid use of your time but most people are loath to talk about this. In fact, talking about your kids on a job interview is one of the things traditionally high on the "Never Mention This" list. One way to do this is to talk about your organizational skills in coordinating activities, running your home, adapting to the changes involved and especially how you have repositioned yourself to be ready to re-enter the workforce. Don't dwell on the cute things your kids do but on how and why you are ready to restart your career and the benefits of hiring someone who is dedicated to creating a balance in their life.

DON'T YOU THINK YOU'RE A LITTLE...?

Overqualified—This word can be code for "too old." Often when interviewers insinuate that you are "overqualified" it is a subtle form of age discrimination. After all, how did you get so qualified? Through years of experience, that's how. Should you point this potentially discriminatory behavior out to them? Only if you are no longer interested in the position. I am not saying that discrimination of any kind should be tolerated, but this is not the time to teach the interviewer a lesson. Once you get the job it would be nice of you to point this potential faux pas out to the interviewer or his boss, as a helpful gesture from a new hire. But pointing this out in the interview is likely to bring the interview to a rapid, though cordial, end. Leading the recruiter to think that you are interviewing just so you can sue the company if they don't hire you is no way to win the position.

Instead, do your best to convince the interviewer that you are completely qualified. You have all the necessary experience and skills and the wisdom to know how to use them. Acknowledge that while you have been doing this function for a number of years, you have kept current in the field. Again, turn the conversation to the things that you want to talk about. Describe all the attributes that you believe the best candidate would have and be sure that you are describing yourself. If the interviewer thinks you are too old for the job, or worse, too old for the organization, describe your work ethic and give examples of how you pace yourself so that you are best able to achieve results. There exists a misperception that older workers are not as facile with technology. Make sure that you share with the interviewer all the latest online search techniques you have used and all the social mediums to which you subscribe. Counter his arguments before he can make them.

Another insidious association of the term overqualified occurs when you are meeting with the hiring manager. Be aware that he might feel threatened hiring someone who appears to have more credentials than he does. In this situation you need to assure him that you are interested in the position for which you have applied, not his. If you have managerial responsibilities reflected on your resume, you may choose to downplay them in the version that you submit for this position. Or you may let on to the manager that yes, you have managed teams similar to this in the past, but that is not your career goal at this time. You are looking for an opportunity to be part of the team and welcome the chance to contribute to another manager's success. You aren't looking for a fast track to the senior office. As they say, you've been there, done that and got the T-shirt.

YOU'VE NEVER DONE THIS BEFORE, HAVE YOU?

No experience in this field—This is the common strike used against career shifters. You may have vast project management experience in the software development field, but what do you know about pharmaceuticals? This is a chance to talk about your transferable skills, the ones that transcend any one industry. The key here is to get the interviewer to recognize the value of the experience that you do have as opposed to focusing on the industry experience you don't. You need to point out the value of the skills and experience you have and demonstrate how your success in another field or industry will equate to success in your new field.

Another element of dealing with the "you have no experience in this industry" issue is to carefully explain your process for choosing this industry or function to switch into. Saying, "The financial industry was drying up so now I've decided to apply myself to pharmaceuticals because people always need medicine and I want to align myself in an industry that is less likely to lay me off," is not going to get you the job. It probably won't even get you a second interview. Some of your transferable skills are your research, analytical and reasoning skills. Explain how you evaluated different industries and companies when choosing which ones to target. Show that this is not a random "I can do anything" approach. Yours is not the infamous "spaghetti on the wall" technique ("I'll just keep throwing my resume out there until it sticks.") but a careful, targeted approach based on solid research and analysis. Use this as an opportunity to outline and explain your process, your conclusions and your implementation strategy based on your research and conclusions. In doing this you demonstrate that you have skills that transfer and translate into success in any industry.

There's a little bit of flattery going on here, but that's okay. The interviewer will be happy to hear that others, particularly outsiders, see his field, and company, as one with a future. Just don't go into complete and obvious toadying up mode.

You may be tempted to overcome the interviewer's concerns by pointing out that you are a fast learner. Perhaps you are, but you are not going to quell fears about your inexperience in the field by reassuring them that you are a fast learner. In fact, this will most likely work against you. The interviewer, particularly if it is the hiring manager or some other line person, may actually take umbrage that you think you can quickly master something that he has taken a lifetime to learn. If you want to impress the interviewer with your ability to pick things up quickly, this is a time to use one of the anecdotes you've prepared. Tell him about a time when you had to take on a new task or responsibility and what you did to get up to speed quickly. He'll get the point. Show him you have done it; don't just tell him that you can. Give concrete examples.

HOW MANY DAYS OFF WILL YOU NEED?

Illegal questions—Plain and simple, it is illegal to ask, in a pre-offer interview, questions about your age, your national origin, your religion or any disability you have or may have had. Questions such as these will secure information that it is illegal and often discriminatory to use in an employment decision.

There are a host of protected categories that are created by federal, state or local laws. Under federal law, employers may not discriminate in hiring based on age, race, sex (including pregnancy), color, religion or national origin. In addition, the Americans with Disabilities Act prohibits discrimination based on disability. Other federal or state statutes make illegal any discrimination in employment based on veteran's status, marital status, sexual orientation or political affiliation.

But rather than turn this into a legal primer (which it most definitely is not), the question is, what do you do when asked questions that may, intentionally or not, be illegal in an employment interview?

Do you point out to the person then and there that the question is illegal and therefore you are not going to answer it? This is not likely to garner you many job offers.

Do you answer the illegal question in hopes that if you don't get hired you'll have grounds to sue the organization later? I hope that you're not going on these interviews seeking fodder for lawsuits.

You could ask the interviewer why they're asking this question that does not seem related to completing the responsibilities of the position for which you are interviewing...but that starts sounding a lot like the first option above and will likely have a similar outcome.

I do not support or advocate the idea of giving in or tolerating discrimination in employment and I hope that's not how you're interpreting this. But if your goal is to get a job then your best bet is to keep your strategic hat on and keep your emotional response (anger, revulsion, disbelief, indignation) in check.

Try to figure out what the interviewer is really concerned about and answer that unasked question. When an interviewer asks an illegal question, either directly ("Is that a wedding ring? Are you married?") or indirectly ("So who did you vote for, Johnson or Goldwater?") they are revealing an underlying concern about you or your potential for success in the position. What you need to do is stay calm and scope out what is on his mind that he is not saying.

This kind of indirect, potentially illegal question is one that women are often asked in interviews. At some point she may be asked about overtime. This is the interviewer's not so subtle attempt to determine if the female candidate has children. Will she be available or will she be running out the door at 4:59? When you get the overtime question simply respond with examples of how and when you have gone the extra mile in previous jobs. If the position involves travel, this is another time when interviewers may cross the line by making assumptions about a woman's ability to meet this requirement of the job. Many women have been asked how their husbands will feel about their having to travel. Whether it is overtime, travel or some other question about your commitment to the job, do your utmost to convince the interviewer that you are able to meet the essential functions of the position.

People who are older or have a visible disability are often questioned about their speed or stamina. Older candidates, who many interviewers believe are too set in their ways, are also questioned about their flexibility, adaptability and ability to master new technologies. Another prejudice lurking just beneath the surface is that older candidates or those with disabilities will cost the company more in benefits and absenteeism. All of these are reflections of biases that exist in the workplace.

I don't advocate bringing a soapbox to your interviews and climbing up on it whenever you recognize an illegal question. The goal is to get a job without sacrificing your principals, ethics or values. Artfully answering illegal questions is a terrific way to demonstrate your business savvy to the interviewer. Address what you identify as the underlying issue to the question and then pause to let it sink in. You will have communicated to the interviewer that you know what he's asking about, but can't ask. And now you have made it clear that you know what his concerns are and have demonstrated that you have met and can continue to meet the challenges of today's workplace. Hopefully, he will recognize that you didn't call him on it or challenge the question. You responded in a professional fashion that is appropriate to the workplace. You have demonstrated yet another of your transferable skills—the ability to control your emotions and stay focused on the goal at hand. For some older (or should I say more experienced?) candidates dealing with ageism, it's great to be able to demonstrate a skill that is developed over years of practice. This is one advantage you have over the less-seasoned competition for the job. Others may have used the most up-to-date technology, but you have mastered something far more valuable—workplace discretion. Use this to the advantage it is. Your years of experience are not a negative in this instance.

IT RHYMES WITH WITCH

Assertiveness—This is a tricky one. Assertiveness is generally regarded as a positive attribute in a candidate. A male candidate, that is. Women sometimes get questioned about their assertiveness because the corporate culture may not be welcoming to strong women. First off, why would you want to work for this company anyway? Any company that can't tolerate strong women is not likely to be in business for very long. But we all know that when a man is assertive he's a strong leader and when a woman is assertive she's a, well, it rhymes with witch. For the same reason that I do not tell my daughter to pretend to be dumber than her boyfriend, I do not advocate that women hide who they are. Questions about assertiveness are often a subtle form of gender discrimination. Play up your leadership qualities but also make it clear that you have been successful working as part of a team. Be clear that you are the kind of person who is not afraid to voice your opinion but demonstrate your workplace diplomacy by citing examples of when you recognized that discretion is the better part of valor. Another of your transferable skills is the ability to scope out a situation and determine the right course of action.

Some men, if they are suspected of being homosexual, are also questioned about their assertiveness. Women are questioned to be sure that they are not too assertive. If the interviewer has concerns about a male candidate's sexual orientation, or is attempting to ascertain a male candidate's orientation, he may ask about the candidate's assertiveness. The interviewer is operating under the misperception that gay men are not assertive. Perhaps he is concerned, if interviewing for a managerial position, that an effeminate male or gay candidate will not be a strong enough personality to do the job. There may be a concern on the part of the interviewer that the staff will be less than open to taking orders from a gay man and that the gay man will not be forceful enough to control the staff. Questions of this nature are no disguise for the bias that lies beneath the surface. If you feel that your assertiveness being questioned has something to do with your sexuality, I do not recommend that you confront the interviewer on this point. I never advocate outright confrontation in the interview. Make it clear that you have the strength and managerial experience to handle a staff and cite examples if you can. Questions about sexual orientation are being deemed illegal in more and

more states, though it is not yet protected by any federal stat-
ute. Remaining closeted is not a sound plan of action, but talking
about your sexual orientation is not advisable for either homosexual or heterosexual candidates. These topics have no place in
the interview. Keep your responses job- and work-related. Answer
the questions clearly and concisely. Brevity in your responses can
be seen as a sign of confidence or assertiveness. Be confident in
your answers and do not drone on endlessly to explain yourself.
Demonstrate your assertiveness in the face of this discriminatory
question. This is a good way to prove that you have the skill in
question.

ARE YOU A "HOPPER"?

Short-term positions—What about answering questions about
previous jobs in which you lasted only a brief time? Many people
have had jobs that lasted only a few months. Should you include a
short-term job on your resume or is it better to leave it out and just
say that you were looking for work? The resume and the application are two different documents, yet they need to be consistent.
You may choose not to include a three- or four-month stint at a
job on your resume but on the application it will ask you, usually in the employment section, to list all employment in reverse
chronological order. If you leave out a briefly held position, you
are going to have a moment of pause, if not outright terror, when it
comes time to sign the application. Because right above your sig-
nature there is a disclaimer stating that all information contained
herein is accurate and truthful to the best of your knowledge. Any
information found to be intentionally false or misstated can and
may be grounds for termination.

It's okay to include short stays with organizations so long as
you have a clear and brief explanation for why the position didn't
work out as you had expected or planned. Be honest when describing your experience at the company, but don't dwell on this facet
of your career too long. It will not, most likely, show you at your

best. Whenever someone doesn't work out in a position there is usually a shared responsibility. Describe why the position didn't work out, accepting that some of the fault may have been yours. Do not put all the blame on the employer, as this will not cast you in the best light to your prospective employer. You might appear to be a whiner or responsibility shirker, neither of which makes you desirable as an employee. Frequent moves do not have the job-hopper stigma that they once did, as long as you have a clear and plausible explanation for the moves. Ideally you will be able to point to a progression of logical moves if you do have several brief assignments on your resume.

YOU CAN'T BE ALL THINGS TO ALL PEOPLE

Lastly, what should you say when you are asked what you do best or what you liked best about your last position, or what you look forward to doing in your next position? Assuming that this is a real question and not just a precursor to "And what did you like least?" you need to have a real answer prepared. Your first instinct might be to say, "I do everything well." Or "I liked everything about my last job!" You're trying to sound upbeat and positive. But this is not the best tactic to use.

At a networking meeting I was talking with an attorney who was looking for work. When I asked him which aspect of the law he preferred, he replied "all of them." He was trying to leave himself open to whatever opportunity presented itself. Employers prefer a more specific response. The interviewers, especially the less experienced ones, are often looking to pigeonhole you into one function. Your broadly framed response is an attempt to not be boxed in. A better way to resist being categorized is to tell the interviewer what you do best or like best while at the same time highlighting a few other strengths you have to offer. You don't want to let others define you, but you have to counter their attempts by making sure that you have defined yourself. Know what you have to offer and then be prepared to "stop on a dime and give them nine cents change." It's great to be flexible and open to any opportunity, but the danger is not stating with assurance and clarity what you want to do or what you have to offer an employer. It may look like you haven't targeted positions carefully enough and make you appear desperate enough to accept anything that comes along. Employers like people who can demonstrate their analytical skills by showing that they have applied those skills to their job search.

THE KEY TO ANSWERING TOUGH QUESTIONS

If you've ever been to a nightclub or cabaret, you may have been impressed at the ease with which the emcee glides from act to act. The filler between performers seems so off-the-cuff and unrehearsed. In point of fact, these transitions are usually prepared and rehearsed long in advance of the moment when you are seeing them. There may be a little ad-libbing, but for the most part, the emcee knew exactly what he was going to say long before he said it. This same approach applies to interviewing and responding to tough questions. You need to have your patter prepared in advance. Remember the word **PATTER** when preparing for an interview.

Prepare your answers in advance whenever possible.

Apply your stories where they will be most effective.

Take the time to determine what the interviewer is really asking about.

Tailor your answers as specifically as possible.

Engage the interviewer in a dialogue to assure that you address concerns.

Respond honestly and completely to the tough questions.

Tough questions in an interview are truly your opportunity to shine. At the outset of the interview you will likely be asked the "ticket of admission" questions—the ones that determine if you have the basic skills and aptitude for the job. The tougher questions are the ones that allow you to separate yourself from the pack. Use these as an opportunity to differentiate yourself from the other candidates and demonstrate why you are the best. Don't try to read the interviewer's mind. Use the success stories from your career to make it clear that you are prepared to handle this position. When you effectively answer the tough questions in the interview, you show that you can handle the tougher challenges of the job.

Eleven

AVOIDING SELF-SABOTAGE

Go confidently in the direction of your dreams

Jobseekers sabotage their job search for a variety of reasons. It's been a long time since you looked for a job and you're not sure how. You were downsized and are insecure. You're not sure if the job is really right for you or if it even exists. You're making a career switch and are not confident in your credibility in your new chosen field.

This chapter is not for everybody. But many people have talked themselves out of applying for jobs, or done things to negate their candidacy. You may be one of them.

The next chapter addresses ways to deal with the stress and emotional toll of being unemployed and looking for a job. In this chapter I want to talk about the different types of self-sabotage some candidates execute during the process.

HOW DO YOU KNOW IF IT'S RIGHT?

Uncertainty is a constant companion during a job search. When you're out of work or trapped in a job that's not fulfilling, you are often plagued with doubt and the fear that you'll never find a job that's right for you.

How do you decide on a new direction? How do you know

what to apply for? The postings look so inviting; it's easy to envision yourself sitting in a pleasant office, surrounded by collegial co-workers, given challenging tasks to complete and the technical support to do your best. But all too often, after you hit send when submitting your resume, you immediately regret having applied.

Then you see a posting and get excited. This is not only a job you can do, but it's actually something that you'd like to do 40 (or more) hours a week. It looks like a good company and the salary fits your budget. You sit down and start to crank out a cover letter. Then the doubts creep in. "What are they hiding? If it's such a great opportunity, why is the position open? Do I really want to do this? The commute's kinda long…" and so on.

Next thing you know, the enthusiasm has drained out of you. Your cover letter, if you even finish it, conveys none of the exhilaration you first felt when you saw the posting. In fact, it's rather uninspired. "I'm responding to your posting that I saw on [fill in your favorite job board]. I feel that I am an excellent candidate for this position because blah, bah, blah." As you reread the letter you doubt that even you'd hire you.

Groucho Marx once said, "I wouldn't want to belong to any club that would have someone like me as a member." That's how you're starting to feel about this potential employer. If you get a response to your submission, you start to wonder even more. How could they possibly respond positively to that letter? They must be pretty hard up to fill this position. By the time you have a phone screen interview, you're about ready to advise everyone you know that if they have stock in this company, they'd better sell because the company is in trouble.

Should you deign to appear at the appointed time of the interview, you may be leaning to one side from that huge chip on your shoulder. Needless to say, you subconsciously sabotage the interview at every turn. Little eye contact. Curt answers. A sinkhole of enthusiasm. You don't get an offer; heck, you probably didn't even get a response after the interview. You're okay with that.

Because you didn't want to work there anyway, did you? You'd made up your mind that you would have turned them down. And you walked away unscathed because you did it to them before they could do it to you. Nope, no hardhearted, unfeeling company is going to hurt you with rejection again.

This example may seem far-fetched, but I've seen it happen time and again. It's a composite of stories I've heard from people who have effectively talked themselves out of jobs. They don't bother to apply, are noncommittal on the phone screen or lose all interest during the interview. Completely qualified individuals do things in interviews that convince the interviewer not to extend an offer.

It's not because of their skills. It's their behavior, their attributes, all the intangibles that so often tip the scales between one candidate and another. While working in recruiting, I heard recruiters selling managers on seemingly lesser-qualified candidates. "Yes, I know that on paper Candidate A seems stronger than Candidate B, but you didn't see Candidate A in the interview. It was very clear that he had very little interest in working here. He was just going through the motions during the interview."

DO ANY OF THESE SOUND FAMILIAR?

Think back on your own interview experiences. Have you ever scuttled your own chances in the way you replied to the interviewer's questions? One person in the Job Support Group told us that she responded to one question saying, "To tell you the truth…" She said from the look on the interviewers face it was clear that he was now wondering what she had said earlier that was not true.

Another person told how she was caught off guard when asked to assess the company's website. She wasn't applying for an IT position and had not bothered to look at anything but the "Careers with [company name]" page. The interviewer was assessing her research skills and she went deer in the headlights on him.

One man in the group was being extraordinarily thorough. His cover letter ran more than two pages. He never got to interview.

Another sent his resume and cover letter as two separate attachments. A cover letter was required, including salary history as well as other information. When he called to follow up he was told that since there was no cover letter, he had not been considered. In the avalanche of applicants, they'd missed his cover letter. Always include your cover letter and resume as a single attachment!

Responding poorly to questions in an interview, not doing your homework, not including a cover letter, and failing to include all the information requested are just a few ways that people sabotage their chances of getting a job.

Self-doubt can creep in and kill your chances at any time in your search. Suddenly, there it is, rearing its vicious head. Snorting smoke from its nose and belching flames from its mouth, this dragon consumes your confidence, your will to pursue opportunities and your belief that you will someday find a suitable position. That's when you need to go back to the questions in Chapter 3 and use the process outlined in this book. This will keep you agile, on target, and will keep that dragon in his cave.

BUILD YOURSELF UP INSTEAD OF BEATING YOURSELF DOWN

Follow the steps in this book. Carefully review what it is that you're looking for in a job. Learn everything you can about the organization. Then you won't find yourself interviewing with a company that is a polar opposite from your ideal. Ask people in your networks about the organization. Do the legwork and you'll keep self-doubt out of your mind, out of your voice and out of your interviews.

Silence the doubts in your head and remember, as Thoreau put it, "If one advances confidently in the direction of his dreams, and endeavors to live the life which he has imagined, he will meet with a success unexpected in common hours."

Twelve

COPING WITH THE STRESS OF LOSING OR FINDING A JOB

I can't take it anymore!

"The moon was a ghostly galleon tossed upon cloudy seas."
Alfred Noyes wrote that line in "The Highwayman" in
1906. About 60 years later songwriter Phil Ochs set the poem to
music. And more than 40 years after that, it's how you feel some
nights when you can't sleep. You are that "ghostly galleon" and
the economy is the "cloudy sea." When business is slow, your job
is frustrating or you can't even get an interview, you lay there
tossing and turning. The image of a storm-tossed sailing ship is
fixed in your mind. You have no control over what will happen.
You are helpless in the face of gale-force winds. You cannot set a
course for success because of circumstances beyond your control.

There are going to be times when business is off or the economy is in a downturn. At these times people's jobs are in jeop-
ardy and freelancers get fewer calls. If you are one of the people
remaining employed while others are released, you are under that
much more pressure to produce.

KEEPING THE DEMONS AT BAY

Being unemployed during a downturn is even scarier than it nor-
mally would be. All you hear about is how bad things are and how

hard it is to get a job. You hear about people accepting positions at half their former salary with fewer benefits. You hear about job searches lasting months or more than a year. How can you remain upbeat and positive in the face of all this? What can you do so that when an interviewer actually calls, you sound like the person that they want to interview? How do you keep the desperation from creeping into your voice?

You can do lots of things during down time to stay active and generate leads. You can write (the web has a voracious appetite for content), update your resume and catch up on your reading. There seems to be an endless supply of things to read, whether it's e-mails, blogs or magazines. Just take care not to become a hermit, spending countless hours staring at your computer screen. Staring at the computer for eight hours a day is not productive job searching.

I also recommend reading the occasional novel or biography. Biographies can be truly inspirational. Most successful people have had to overcome some pretty bad times.

But reading and blogging doesn't generate income. You're going to have to get out from behind that screen and network. Attend meetings (free ones are the best), call people to see if they have any new or recurring needs and do whatever you can to market yourself. Running a job support group for people who are in transition is one way that I keep in touch with people and their issues. At the same time that I'm volunteering and helping others, I often feel that I'm getting as much out of the meetings as those attending. That's because volunteer work can be a surprisingly effective way to network. I know someone who lost his job due to the attacks on 9/11. To get himself to stop thinking about his own problems he volunteered, doing whatever he could as close to Ground Zero as possible. He didn't do this to network, but he was amazed at the people he met and the connections he made. I'll tell you this: he hasn't been out of work much since those days.

PUT IT IN WRITING

If you're a freelancer, writing is one of the best, if solitary, uses of down time. The problem is, when you don't have much work it's hard to get motivated or feel creative. You feel depressed. That's when Solitaire and other computer games seem most alluring. Being depressed tends to staunch the flow of creative juices. Force yourself. Don't dedicate a whole day to writing. I can't imagine doing it for six or eight hours a day. But I can imagine doing it for 30 minutes. When I sit down to write, I always say, "I'll just throw down a few ideas for 30 minutes or so." Invariably at least an hour goes by, sometimes more. It's not all good, but it's kind of like taking pictures of your newborn baby during the first year of her life. You're going to take hundreds, if not thousands, of pictures. You know that 97% of them will be awful. I have lots of pictures of my kids turning away, making a face, or spitting up. But I have a few beauties. That's what it's like with writing. Put it all down and a few nuggets will appear.

Writing is also a great way to get your name out in front of your industry. Suddenly you're not unemployed, you're an expert. When you're asked about what you've been doing since your last job, you can point to articles you've written. If asked what you've done to stay current, point to the research and its product, your articles. This is a very positive statement to make. You weren't sitting around focusing solely on your job search; you were feeding both sides of your brain.

One of the best ways to avoid isolation to do is call someone. Reaching out in e-mail is similar, but is not the same. I can tell you that being a consultant is sometimes a lonely game. So is being unemployed. Sometimes you can't even share your fears or concerns with your spouse or life partner because you don't want them to worry, especially if you're the main breadwinner. But others will understand. Other people who are unemployed know what you're going through. Members of my support group have expressed their fears in meetings and then point out that they can't say these things to their spouse. Some bring up the pressure they feel from their partners. It helps to talk with others who are experiencing the same things you are.

When you work alone, either as a consultant or a job seeker—and especially if you were previously part of a large organization—it can be very isolating and that's hard to handle. Dealing with every facet of your business is hard. Dealing with the pressures of being unemployed and looking for a job is harder. You need someone to talk with, to bounce ideas off, to have a cup of coffee with. It's great when you can put a positive spin on things, but sometimes it's okay just to call because things aren't so great. Just don't get into an extended pity party. I have a freelancer friend who calls weekly to complain that she doesn't have enough work. I gently point out that calling me is not networking. She needs to call people who can hire her.

If you're a freelancer, it's hard to call someone and admit that business is lousy. What if the person you call is flourishing? You may wind up feeling even worse. But everyone has had a slump (and that's all it is) and we all know what it's like. And if you call someone with lots of work, who knows, they may have some for you.

USE YOUR NETWORKS

One of the things to do is to build two networks. A Revenue Generating Network (RGN) and a Support Network (SN). The RGN is the one that you should be calling, and should want to call. But sometimes you need to call someone in the SN before you call the RGN. That way if you get someone who can hire you on the phone you won't sound too needy or desperate.

Your SN includes friends, family, clergy, other people seeking jobs, members of your support group, or a career counselor. For freelancers, your network includes other freelancers. None of us got where we are by ourselves, and just about everyone can find a few minutes to listen and empathize because we've all been there at one point or another. And as the saying goes, "There but for the grace of God…"

Your RGN is more extensive. A lot of the same people who are in your SN are also in your RGN because you never know where a lead will come from. But now you will include friends of friends, former employers, prospective employers, people you've met at conferences or networking meetings, and just about anyone who you can talk to about what you have to offer an organization. There will be times when you need to be a little shameless in promoting yourself to others. You must be ready with your pitch, sometimes called your "elevator speech." This is your 15- to 30-second synopsis of what you have to offer. Your elevator speech should not be a summary of your resume or work history. Prospective employers or leads are not interested in what you've done for others. They want to know what you can do for them!

How do you deal with the financial stress? You're out of work and you don't have money coming in. Perhaps you're working but you're not making enough to make ends meet. Maybe you've started a new venture but there's nothing coming in yet, or you're a freelancer and clients are slow to pay. Any one of these is enough to keep you up nights, and frequently you are suffering more than one at a time.

Some people will urge you to take a "survival" job to ease the financial stress. Any job just so long as you are bringing in some income. "It's good for your self-esteem," they'll say, and "It's easier to find a job when you have a job." Both statements are true, but these are nothing more than platitudes that may have little relevance to your current situation. Going to work is good for your self-esteem—unless you have to drag yourself there each day. Working in a very low-level position can actually erode your self-esteem. A lot depends on the type of person you are. Sure it's easier to get a job when you have a job, but how do you spin the positive side of working in a job usually filled by a high-school student? You can make it clear that you needed to do something to generate income, but this can backfire if the interviewer perceives your choice differently or negatively.

You need to determine the impact of taking a certain amount of time away from your job search. Going to work at any job will sap a certain amount of your energy. It may make it more difficult for you to schedule networking meetings or interviews, especially if the survival job does not afford much flexibility. Will you walk into a job interview ashamed of your survival job? If the answer is yes, then filling your days with an "any" job may hurt you more than it helps. No matter how much you hone your interview skills, if you are hiding something, you are going to set off alarms in the mind of your interviewer. A good interviewer will work that much harder to determine what else is going on in your work history that you might be hiding. Whether or not to seek and secure a survival job is a very individual decision that only you, with the input of your Personal Board of Directors, or at the very least the input of your partner, can make.

You also need to consider medical insurance coverage, which for many is the deciding factor. If Cobra has been exhausted or you have difficulty affording an individual plan, you might need to get a survival job just to secure benefits. This is a reality many are facing in today's economic climate.

STRESS-BUSTERS

There are lots of things you can do to relieve the stress. The first is: Be kind to yourself. Stop beating yourself up. You're not a failure and most likely you didn't bring this on yourself. Some people punish themselves, which inhibits their ability to get past the depression. Then not only are they out of work, but they can't have any fun. Along with working your networks, you need to look for other things that you can do, things that you like to do, to get out of this rut.

One thing some people do to get out of a depression is watch funny movies. This is no time to put *Titanic* into the DVD player.

Find something that will make you laugh in spite of yourself. And there's no need to sign up for Netflix or visit the local video store. Most libraries have ample video collections. Or ask your friends for recommendations and loaners. This accomplishes another goal. It allows you to talk to people instead of becoming a recluse. Here's another misperception we may have when we get depressed: "I'm unemployed. No one wants to see me or talk to me or associate with me. They're afraid it will rub off." Keep reaching out to people, especially those in your Support Network.

Doing volunteer work or mentoring someone are great ways to sharpen your skills and feel useful. Helping someone else is a wonderful use of your time and will remind you that you do have a lot to offer to people. And once again, it gets you out with people. You're not going to find a job or your next assignment by endlessly scrolling through Craigslist. You have to get out there. When you get back to your computer refreshed and feeling a bit more energized, you may be surprised that opportunities that you talked yourself out of before now look pretty good.

Another way to get out among people, expand your network and sharpen your networking and job search skills is to join—or create—a support group. There are lots of them at churches, synagogues, and community centers. There are also "professional" groups such as the Five O'Clock Club or 40Plus. Your local Chamber of Commerce is another source. More positively, form you own. This is a great way to demonstrate leadership skills and attract people to you, which again expands your network. All of these activities are time consuming, but have a much greater payoff than watching the soaps. LinkedIn, a business-oriented social networking site, is another wonderful resource to find networking groups in your area, or as a launching pad to forming your own.

This chapter has dealt with your mental and emotional health, but don't overlook your physical health. Exercise, yoga, and meditation are just a few of the things you can do to make it easier to handle all that you are going through, whether it is a seemingly never-ending search or dealing with a difficult boss. Release those endorphins. When you feel good physically, it's easier to feel good mentally. I know lots of people who break up their day with a brisk walk, summer or winter, rain or shine. Some days, this is the only structured and defined activity in their day.

Kevin Durkin, an Iyengar certified yoga teacher in Denver, Colorado, says that, "Any exercise is good for you, but conscious exercise is better." He points out that yoga is to be practiced, not perfected. When you practice yoga, it is not a competition sport at which you are trying to beat someone else. You're learning how to be present in the moment.

When you exercise, think about what you're doing. Don't let your mind wander to everything that's worrying you. Kevin once described a stockbroker on his exercise bike every morning with *The Wall Street Journal* open in front of him. Although the exercise was good, he wasn't in touch with what his body was feeling and therefore he wasn't reaping the full rewards of his exercise. The mind and the body were on separate planes.

To get the most out of any exercise program, whether it is yoga, running or working out at the gym, focus on what you are doing and feeling at that moment. Leave all the other stuff outside. Kevin says that yoga is "training the mind to be present." You are creating a positive feedback loop. This sense of calm and focus is something that will help you enormously when you are out pounding the pavement in search of an interview. And when you land that interview, you'll be more focused on the interviewer's questions and your mind will be more nimble in your answers. Have you ever left an interview and slapped yourself in the forehead thinking, "Oh, I forgot to tell them about the campaign I designed for that major client!" or "I should have told them about the time I saved the whole project by catching the flaw in the program!" That will happen less frequently if you become adept at shutting out distractions and keeping present in the moment.

In his song, "Some Kind of Hero," reknowned singer-song-writer David Roth writes,

> I have discovered that worrying works
> I'll tell you why I'm sure
> Most of the things that I worry about
> Never even come close to occur.

When you worry you are generating negative energies, usually about things that will never happen. You are "prepaying" on pain. You are feeling awful about what might happen. You need to live in the moment.

It is so easy to get depressed when you are job seeking. The activity is filled with rejection that often leads people to self-destructive behaviors. You often feel so out of control when job hunting; you need to find things that you can control. Your exercise schedule is one of the constants you can place on your daily schedule to combat the feeling of helplessness. Besides, when you were working and overstressed, you probably made a New Year's resolution at some point to exercise more, eat better and take better care of yourself. Now you have the time. You don't need a fancy gym membership—in fact that can be counterproductive if you are also stressed out about money. Go to the library and take out an exercise DVD. Then use it!

One of the most important things to remember is that you are not alone. If you're a freelancer or you're unemployed, it is very easy to let your world collapse in around you. You lie awake all night and then you can't focus during the day. You imagine that you are the only one who has ever gone through this. You don't know who to talk to and if you did you wouldn't know what to say. This is only one of the vicious cycles you need to break in order to find your way out of this malaise. To reset your course toward whatever your ultimate goal is. Whether it is more revenue, a better job, or finding the next job, you need to get yourself into the right frame of mind to successfully find that safe harbor.

Be kind to yourself.

Thirteen

STAYING POWER

What can I do to keep my job now that I have one?

Ask any professional athlete and they'll tell you that it is just as hard, if not harder, to stay in the big leagues as it was to get there in the first place. In Chapter Two I talked about the things you can do to keep out of the crosshairs of a downsizing when your company is restructuring. Now you need to develop strategies to insure you stay in your job once the music stops and all the seats are allotted.

This is not as simple as it sounds.

I worked with Hal, a member of The Job Support Group who had spent more than ten years as a freelancer. For personal reasons Hal started looking for a job within an organization as a salaried employee. After working with me for a few months he secured a position in his very specialized audit function. He has held this job for more than three years, and the entire time he has been there he has been under extreme pressure to produce, reduce and deduce. That's produce results, reduce the time it takes to produce them, and deduce what the heck his manager wants from him (Hal's manager is not a champion communicator). He's continued to come to the support group on occasion, even though he's been employed, for help in dealing with the acute pressure under which he's had to operate.

THE RIF MYTH

Countless organizations think that the surest path to profitability is to reduce headcount. Yet a Bain & Company study of layoffs at S&P 500 firms has shown that few organizations reap the expected benefits from cutting heads. In fact, it took these firms 6 to 18 months to realize savings from job cuts. When calculating savings, most executives fail to account for the added cost of recruiting, hiring and training new people who will be needed when good times return. Companies often find that they need to hire—or rehire—people as soon as the business climate shifts. Other surveys have found that most restructuring efforts fall far short of the objectives originally established for them. One found that only 46% of the companies surveyed said their cuts reduced expenses enough. The most frequently cited reason for failing to meet the expense reduction goal? Four times out of five, managers ended up replacing some of the very people they had dismissed. Often the new employees are hired at salaries higher than the salaries of the people who were released, further eroding any savings that had been realized. Imagine the impact on the psyche of those employees who were retained during the staff cuts if they hear through the rumor mill that the new employees were brought in at substantially higher salaries. Hiring managers often kid themselves into believing that the employees won't find out.

The impact of cutting and hiring, churning the workforce, is enormous. The negative impact on productivity and profitability is obvious but rarely traced back to a flawed decision to reduce headcount. Invariably, when the savings are not realized, management comes to the conclusion, "We didn't cut deeply enough. We were trying to be nice. Now we have to be really ruthless."

CAREER CRAFTING

You want to be sure that you are not considered expendable and fall victim to a "last in, first out" mindset. You can take many approaches to make sure that management recognizes you for the valued asset you are. We keep hearing senior managers saying, "People are our most important asset." And then they swing the axe indiscriminately. What's a worker to do?

It's simple. Do your job. As well as you possible can.

There are many ways to interpret that last sentence. You think, "I'm going to make myself indispensable. I'll make myself so valuable they'll never let me go." How do you plan to go about this? Will you learn every single job in the place so you are the ultimate "swingman," able to step in for anyone? Will you hoard information so that you are the "keeper of the keys to the kingdom"? Perhaps your plan is to hitch your wagon to the star of the highest person in the organization chart that you can reach. None of these plans is foolproof, and in fact most are seriously flawed. Yet this is what I hear people telling me they're doing to insure their continued employment.

Jobs today are fluid. You can't expect to do just one thing. Most likely you will be called upon to fill many roles no matter where you work. The people who are most valued today are the ones who are able to craft their career and carve a path. There are five keys to getting and keeping a job today and you're going to have to hack your way through the jungle to find, get and keep your position.

Why the machete references? Because the word I want you to remember is CARVE. This is an acronym for Competent, Aligned, Results, Versatile, and Engaged. Employers want, need and value employees who embody these traits.

Competent. You need to know how to do your job. You need to be skilled so that you can do your job as it exists today and also stay aware of trends so you can adapt and do it better tomorrow. The one constant is change and nobody does their job the same way today that they did five, two or often even one year ago. That's why competency rules. Not perfection. In the first place, nobody can do their job perfectly all the time (although I am rooting for airline pilots to come very close to this benchmark). But perfection takes a long time to achieve and by the time you have mastered the perfect way to do your job, the requirements have changed. You are expected to be competent at all facets of your job—the tactical aspects as well as the strategic ones. This means you have to know all the software and you also need to understand the so-called intangible skills like teamwork, adaptability, and the ability to recognize the critical tasks and prioritize your time accordingly. These are the skills that will make you successful. It's more than simply doing your job well, it's doing all the taken-for-granted things that make you the "employee of choice." You may have heard of the "employer of choice." We all want to work for that company. Make yourself the "employee of choice."

Competence is the first key, because without that nothing else matters. Your first responsibility is to make sure that you know how to do your job and that you do it well. If you're not getting the job done, no one will care how versatile you are.

Doing it well does not mean doing it up to your standards. To do the job well it is critical that you are clear on your boss's expectation of the position. You may be the most gifted graphic designer on the planet, but if your efforts are not in sync with the needs of the organization, the client or your manager's expectations for performance, you're going to find yourself back in the earlier chapters of this book. One of the most important competencies, and you're going to see this in virtually every job posting, is "excellent communication skills." Use these skills to insure that you understand completely what is expected of you so that you're able to deliver. One of the key questions to ask your manager is, "What will you see when this job is done completely and correctly?" Be careful because your manager may not even have thought this through himself. Engage your manager in a discussion about the desired outcomes of the project before you get knee deep in the swamp. Then remember to check back with your manager frequently, because as you know, projects and expectations can change as frequently as a runway model.

I'm talking about **Alignment**. Aligning your efforts, your work, with the goals and expectations of the organization, manager or client.

There isn't room for "lone rangers" in today's workforce. There may be times when you are called to complete work individually, but even then the projects to which you are assigned are part of a whole. Successfully meeting your performance objectives supports the goals of the department, division or organization. Ideally there will be a clear line of sight from your efforts to the overall success of the organization. At one organization I worked with, the big push one year was "Customer Focus." At a kick-off meeting, someone from the back office said he had no interaction with customers. He was back office. The answer from the podium was, "If you're not serving the customer, you're serving someone who is." This is alignment in its simplest form.

To be considered valuable, you need to, as much as possible, make sure that the work you are doing is clearly and obviously aligned with the most important work of the organization. That's why just being good, or competent, is not enough. You may be the best at what you do, but if you are working at cross currents with the efforts of the organization, it will go unrecognized or worse, be seen as an unnecessary expense. During the mid-20th century, AT&T had a mission of Universal Service. This meant a telephone in every American home and business at an affordable cost. If you were working on something that did not move AT&T closer to this goal, you could expect to be challenged why you were doing what you were doing. AT&T reinforced its mission with its actions. The goal of Universal Service did not simply mean selling a phone to every possible customer, it meant maintaining the service. In the event of a natural disaster or labor shortage, everyone in management assumed line responsibilities until service was restored. This is alignment in a higher form.

Alignment of goals and efforts is another key to staying in the job you've fought so hard to get. This usually means being able to explain how the successful completion of your goal moves the organization closer to its vision. Ideally you will be able to give this explanation in just a few sentences. In its highest form alignment means frequent contact with your manager and her manager as well. Goals change. Projects get redesigned, restructured and refocused. You cannot work in a bubble, assuming that what you were told in January will still be true in June. Do not think that your objectives have been carved in stone. Alignment often includes defining and then redefining those goals. This is the key to proper alignment. Imagine you're driving a car. Try making a quick maneuver or going around a corner at high speeds if the tires were not properly aligned. You'd chew those radials right off. Managing change in an organization has often been likened to changing the tires on a car going 60 MPH. If you are not constantly ensuring that your efforts are aligned with those of the organization, you very likely will be left on the side of the road.

Results, or having a results focus, a bottom line mentality, is the next piece of the keeping-your-job puzzle. Sure you're competent and you've carefully aligned what you're doing with the objectives of the organization. But what have you done for me lately? What have you achieved?

To keep your job you must produce measurable results. I can't put it any more simply. You must reach the final outcome. Captain Kirk's mission was not just to explore the final frontier, it was to report back on what he found. It was more than just to "boldly go where no man has gone before." It was also to come back and do something with the information! I was once debating the difference between measurement and reporting with a colleague. She maintained that they were one and the same. My feeling is that measurement is an interim goal of reporting. Collecting accurate data is measurement. Making sure you are collecting the correct data is a second part of the process. Interpreting that data is reporting. If I collect reams of information but do not analyze and interpret that data into a cohesive recommendation, then I have not contributed fully to the process.

One thing you can rely on in business today is that everyone is busy. Usually the person who has asked for the report thinks that she is busier than you. Handing in incomplete information or raw data is not going to impress anyone. You have to reach a conclusion. You must produce results.

Your results must be aligned to achieve success. Producing results that do not support the greater goals of the organization will not win you any points. The key to insuring that you are focusing on the right results again comes back to alignment; open and frequent communication with your manager. You cannot be afraid to ask questions, especially when you are new on the job. Constantly reaffirm that you are putting your energy in the right direction. Many times you will find yourself working project to project. Traditional departments in which you work for months or years on end with the same group of people doing the same function are becoming less and less common. Each time you are assigned to a new work team or task force, it is incumbent on all the members of the team to identify the interim and final outcomes that the team is expected to produce. Equally important are the standards for the outcomes. It's not just what you produce, but also the quality of your results. If it's data, it must be accurate. If it's a machine, it must work. If it's software, it should be bug-free. And if it's a jet engine, it better be perfect. When you are clarifying management's expectations of what must be accomplished, be sure you understand the standards for performance whether they are defined in terms of quality, timeliness, or volume.

Versatility is the next key to sticking around. Once upon a time the saying was, be a jack-of-all-trades and a master of one. Today you need to be a jack-of-all-trades and a master of some. Previously I explained that many hiring managers are reluctant to make a hiring decision because they get so few opportunities to do so that they are afraid to make a mistake. Having the versatility to fill more than just the basics of the job description will not only help you to get a job, but also to keep one. Candidates who only have the "ticket of admission" skills will get some consideration, but the ones who exceed the minimum requirements are the ones who get the offers. The same holds true once you are on the job.

Organizations can rarely afford specialists anymore. With all the projects and task forces to which you will be assigned, you need to bring a full portfolio of different competencies. This is why it is so important to take the time to assess your skills and find the holes in your skill set. Again, this ties back to the alignment idea. What is the direction of your organization? What skills will be in demand over the next 6 or 12 or 18 months? Do you have them? How much time do you have to develop them? How do you most effectively integrate new ideas, new information and new concepts?

The most common way for people to learn new skills is on the job. But what if you are trying to master a new skill as part of a career switch? I worked with a man named Jon who was making a fairly radical switch from working with computers and telecommunications to working in facilities. He thought of himself as someone who learned best on the job. He had some knowledge of what facilities people were expected to do from his work in telecommunications installations. But he had no real capital "F" facilities work on his resume. He was pretty good with his hands, but how was he going to convince someone to take a chance on him and give him the kind of job he wanted next?

The strategy we devised was twofold. The first was to redesign Jon's resume from a chronological to a functional one that highlighted his transferable skills. We needed to show employers that he had the ability to accomplish results in this role and draw parallels between the installations he had done and the more comprehensive facilities projects he'd have to undertake. Second, we targeted smaller organizations that assigned greater value to his versatility and competency. A smaller organization would be more willing to take a chance on someone who was relatively unproven, yet had tremendous potential. He found a job with an organization that needed a facilities manager with in-depth knowledge of telecommunications. The depth of his telecommunications knowledge made up for his lack of facilities experience. A one-year contract has evolved into a multi-year assignment.

To some degree, many people are on-the-job learners. They need to do something in order to fully understand it and be able to do it on their own. Others learn best through self-paced learning at a computer or from a manual. For still others, traditional classroom instruction is best. You need to identify your learning style. Think back to the last time you had to master a new procedure or technique. How did you accelerate the learning process? What kinds of things did you do to ensure that you understood what was expected of you and how to do it? The most valuable people are the ones who are competent, aligned, results-oriented and versatile not only in their abilities but in their ability to assimilate large amounts of new information quickly. That is something that you will be expected to do on the job whether you are new or a longer-tenured employee. Even if you don't change jobs, the way the objectives of the position are met will change. You have to be a quick learner.

Almost everyone thinks that they're a quick learner. I can think of countless interviews when I asked the candidate about his or her ability to do something that I had a sense he or she had no idea how to do. Invariably, once it was established that the candidate had no experience in the area I was probing, the candidate volunteered, "But I'm a quick learner." My next question was, "How do you like to learn?" and I would follow that up by asking them for an example of a time when they had to master a new skill in a short period of time and how they did it. I was able to determine pretty quickly if the candidate really was a quick learner. Your versatility needs to extend beyond what you can do now to what you will be able to do in the future. That kind of versatility is often called potential.

One cautionary comment about versatility though. Be sure that you are, as I said, a master of some functions. You don't want to become so versatile that you are not perceived as being a "key player" in any one area. You don't have to be a superstar, but you want to avoid the label of utility player as well. Utility players have great value to an organization because they are the ones who can step in anywhere. But often these are the people who are seen as expendable when management does start to look to reduce headcount. So make versatility one of your strengths but not your primary value. Use the breadth of your knowledge and skills as one of the retention tools in your portfolio, but don't stake your hopes solely on your versatility.

Another benefit of versatility is the ability to create the job you really want. It's very rare that people are hired into their dream jobs. More often than not, especially in the current market, people are willing to take almost any job. One of the keys to sticking around is to take the job that is offered and then start turning it into the job that you want. Let people know of the other things that you can do, the other skills you possess. Whenever possible, make sure that these are the kinds of skills that are in short supply in your organization. Pretty soon you will find that you are being asked more and more frequently to do those things that you are good at and like to do, and less and less to do the onerous tasks you might have been hired to do. I know a trainer who was offered a position as an instructional designer. She took the job because it was a good company and a good opportunity to work with talented and friendly people. Within a year of starting, when working with the trainers who would be delivering the classes she was designing, it became pretty evident to her new employer that she knew an awful lot about classroom facilitation. She was far more than just a subject matter expert; she was a gifted presenter. No organization is going to let that kind of skill atrophy on the sidelines. It wasn't long before she found herself balancing her time between instructional design and delivery. She has other as yet untapped skills and while the responsibility for designing classes will never go away entirely, she has built up an admirable array of measurable and highly visible assets. I think she will be with this company for quite some time. She certainly produced significant results, but her versatility, the breadth of what she has to offer, cements the deal. Further, her excitement for what the position has morphed into has made her even more in demand. She looks forward to getting to work in the morning. She is fully engaged in what she is doing and with the company for which she does it.

Engaged is one of the most frequently heard buzzwords today when referring to employees. Organizations no longer just want talented, productive employees; they want employees who care about the organization and its product. Management has realized that when employees care about the work of the organization, they are more productive and tend to turn out higher-quality products. As Bill Catlette and Richard Hadden made clear in their book *Contented Cows Give Better Milk*, creating a satisfied, fully engaged workforce is the key to any organization's financial security. They quote former chairman and CEO of Procter & Gamble Owen (Bud) Butler, who said, "Productivity comes from people, not machines."

What does it mean to be engaged? Are you supposed to walk up to your boss each morning and express your delight at being able to work for him? Not really. There's another name for that type of behavior, and it's not one you want. Engaged employees are the ones who demonstrate all the keys I've been talking about. They are skilled, versatile people whose efforts are aligned with the goals of the organization to achieve results. They seem to have achieved a positive work/life balance, which often translates as someone who could walk into work every morning with a smile on her face thinking how happy she is to have this job, and not just for the paycheck. Much like the woman I described above. There really are people who can't wait to get to work every day because they are excited about picking up where they left off the day before. It's more than simply being able to provide for your family. It's more than being thankful you have health benefits. It's a feeling that what you are doing means something. That doesn't mean your organization must be working on a cure for cancer or finding shelter for people who are homeless. People just like to feel that they are making a contribution to something; that their work matters. Think of it as the "Anti-Dilbert."

Sometimes a job is just a job. Sometimes a job is your identity. If you want to increase your chances of staying in the job you have, it helps if the position can be both your vocation and avocation. I don't mean that you need to be doing it 24 hours a day. But your vocation is your employment and your avocation is very often the other things that you do in your life, the things you truly care about. Can you find a way to care about your work as the source of more than just a paycheck?

I remember when I was in graduate school and spoke with classmates about what we wanted to do with our degrees after graduation. Most people wanted to find jobs in different industries. A few were hoping that the degree would be the key to advancement within their current organization. When we fantasized, we talked about being cutting-edge. We talked about creative firms —advertising, publishing and information technology. Nobody mentioned financial firms, banks or insurance companies. After I spoke at graduation, I was approached by a representative of what was at the time the sixth-largest bank in the country. He was scouting for talent and, no surprise; he made a beeline for the graduate who had been at the podium. It happened to be me. But a bank? My background was in arts administration. This was not what I had planned.

Cut to the chase, I took the job. I'd invested a lot in the degree and needed to start earning it back. So I took a job with a bank. But not only was I working for a bank, I was working in the human resource department that supported the back offices of the bank. Loan processing, check processing, Wholesale Day-of-Deposit Accounts. Where was the glamour? I felt pretty far from the cutting edge.

To care about this job, I needed to think hard about what it was we did at the bank. What did a bank enable people to do? It's often said that an organization is heavily influenced by its product. If you work in publishing, you're likely to find a lot of literate people who love books and want to be involved in the production or distribution of them. If you work in broadcasting, you are likely to work with people who are passionate about communications. Banks make money with money. How was I going to get engaged in that? I spent a lot of my first year talking with the people in the lines of business our HR department supported. I found out about the small businesses that would not stay open without the letters of credit we provided. I learned about the people who were able to buy homes because of the mortgages we processed. I thought about all the things that people rely on banks to do or provide, and I started to feel a swell of pride to be working there. I became engaged.

Before working at the bank, I worked for the kind of organization you would think people would be very engaged in—a non-profit social service agency that provided arts exposure to people in hospitals, nursing homes, shelters and prisons. This is exactly the kind of place that people dedicate their lives to. But I became burned out. I worked there for eight years. At the end of my tenure I was taking more pride in how well-run my department was than in the actual services that we provided. When you find yourself more involved in the minutiae of the daily life of the office than in the greater goals of the organization, you may want to start checking for other signs of burnout.

Maybe you took your current job because you had been out of work for the past 6, 9 or 12 months. Maybe you had exhausted all the credit available and had to compromise and take the first offer you got. Maybe you just got fed up with all the self-assessment exercises the career coaches were making you take and in your frustration said, "I'm just going for the next paycheck I can get." But now you are in the job. To stay there on your terms, you need to find a way to make it more palatable. You need to find a way to get excited about where you work and what you're doing, or the choice of whether you stay or not will be taken out of your hands. You may be competent, versatile and aligned, but employers want more. They want your head and your hands, but they also want your heart. More and more they realize that your engagement is the key to their success.

WHICH ELEMENT OF CARVE CARRIES THE MOST WEIGHT?

You may be wondering which of these five attributes is most important. It would be easy to say, "All of them." But that would be disingenuous on my part. There is a hierarchy to these but in the same way that jobs are fluid, so are the on-the-job demands you face. Which of these five elements will be most important in keeping you employed depends on a number of external factors. Part of your task now that you are employed is to keep your antennae honed and remain sensitive to what's going on in the organization, so you know which element of CARVE to emphasize at any given time.

Competence never goes out of style. I've never heard anyone complain that someone was too good at their job. You don't want to be seen as investing to much time in developing unnecessary skills, but similar to the theory that you can't be too rich or too thin, you can't be too good. Make sure you know what's expected of you today, and anticipate tomorrow's requirements. One of your competencies needs to be forecasting the direction of the work of your department.

Alignment is critical because that's how you ensure that you are working on those aspects of your job that are most important. When prioritizing your efforts, you need to know what's going on so that you are not aligning your energy with last year's, or last week's, objective. If you should find yourself in a more static environment, then this will be less important. But most industries and organizations that I've come in contact with are anything but static. In fact, most organizations are very busy reinventing themselves. Expect the ability to align your efforts to remain paramount among your skills.

Results, strangely enough, can vary in importance. At some point you will be called upon to produce something, but in certain areas, R&D for instance, you might have a longer lead time to come up with something. In many pharmaceutical companies, the time it takes to develop and bring a new drug to the market can be years. So in this instance the product might be less important than the process. But don't interpret that to mean results don't matter. What gets measured gets managed. And what gets managed is what gets done. Management will always be looking for people who can produce high-quality results, especially those workers who can maintain a focus on results in times of flux. But that's when you start looking back at alignment.

Versatility depends a lot on your organization's size. The larger the organization, the more you can afford to specialize. In small organizations your versatility may be the key to your survival. Versatility may even trump competence in importance in a small organization. It's also very important if your organization is going through any kind of restructuring. Versatility can be the key to keeping your job through a merger or acquisition as well. So those are times to play up this strength.

Engagement, because it is one of the newer terms being used to describe the ideal employee, is getting a lot of prominence these days. But because it is new, it is defined differently, and sometimes misunderstood, in many organizations. Being engaged in your work and the work of your organization is very important if loyalty is one of the values of the organization. In comparison to results, however, engagement often pales. I've heard managers say that they don't care if you're engaged or not so long as you get the work done. When the rubber hits the road, engagement may be the first attribute jettisoned. But don't minimize employee engagement. As the competition stiffens, you will find that almost everyone you meet in the workplace is competent, in alignment, produces great results and is versatile. Your level of engagement might be the one thing that tips the balance in your favor. Plus, an engaged employee is often a happy employee, and a happy employee tends to achieve better results than an unhappy one.

So yes, each of the employee attributes is important. Since organizations are so fluid you need to bring all five to the table. You can't rely on one because tomorrow things might change and you'll need to play up another attribute. The key to increasing your staying power is to keep the lines of communication open with your manager and her manager, with your co-workers and with both the internal and external environment. This way you'll know how to carve out your position and defend your job.

It may be a jungle out there, but you are equipped with the tools and the knowledge to tame it and carve out a career.

Fourteen

SO NOW WHAT HAPPENS

How do I put all this to use?

So now what happens. You're going to get a job. Someday, and maybe someday soon. You're not going to stay unemployed forever, although some days it may feel that way. You're mastering a critical skill for this especially difficult time but a skill that will serve you today and forever. You will never again be fearful of losing your job because you know that you've learned how to find one.

IT'S YOUR TURN

You know how to navigate the flood of emotions. You know how to build your networks. You know how to dissect the job market and find jobs before they're posted. You know how to make yourself marketable, presentable and desirable.

You've learned how to behave on an interview and how to recognize trap questions. You understand the importance of following up and not getting discouraged when you don't hear anything. You know to use your support network as well as your revenue generating network.

You, you, you. It's all about you.

And the time is now. Now, now, now.

Now is the time to make those calls, work your network, answer those ads. Now while you're excited and inspired. Now while you believe in yourself. Now before the roller coaster takes another dip. Because there will be swoops and turns but you can start to enjoy the ride because you've asked all those questions and come up with answers. You have a clearer idea of what you're going to be next. The reinvention process is under way and the new invigorated you is going to emerge from the tunnel.

This is the moment you've been waiting for and building toward. You're closer than ever to nailing that interview and getting that job. You've worked so hard. This is the time to put all your plans into motion. Someone's gonna get hired. It might as well be you.

If there are gaps in your plan, don't worry. You'll fill them. If you need another link in your network, you'll find it. Just the same way you built the rest of your network. Connection to connection to connection. Someone you already know knows the person you need to reach. You just have to follow the dots to get to that person. You know how to do this.

If you're preparing for an interview, you know the types of questions the interviewer will likely use and how best to answer. You know the anecdotes from your past that exemplify your best traits and how to work these into the conversation. You know how to make the interview a conversation, how to build rapport with the interviewer so she can picture you as a productive member of their team. You know how to effectively close the interview and the tactics for following up, including ways to get past the gatekeeper after the interview.

If you're depressed, call someone in your support network. If you're elated, call someone in your revenue generating network. If you've just made a connection with someone you've been trying to reach, or landed an interview or a job, share the news with someone else in your support group. Let them know that there is hope. There is a light at the end of the tunnel and it isn't the headlight of an oncoming train. Let them know the system works.

This system works. Take the time to figure out what you want to do. Maybe it's a derivative of what you used to do. Maybe it's what you always wanted to do but didn't think you could take the chance. The chance has been given to you. Use this gift. Use your energy and intellect to identify the best market for your skills and talents. Create a resume and craft a cover letter that opens doors and gets recruiters interested in meeting you. Learn all you can about an organization before you reach out to it. Make the system work for you.

EVERYTHING'S OKAY

Finding a new job is something almost half the workforce is going to go through at some point in their work life. The days of one job, one company until you get the gold watch are gone forever. You must be in control of your career. You must craft your career. It is a living organism that will need tending on a regular basis. You can't allow others to decide what your career should look like. You can't afford to let your career just happen. You are not a rudderless sailboat being blown about in the breeze. Chart your course. Make your choices, but be prepared to make midcourse corrections. You'll make mistakes. You'll make a few poor choices along the way. That's okay. Learn from them and move on. Don't dwell on what went wrong, but take from the experience what was right and build on that. There is no wasted experience. I read that someone once said, "Everything ends up O.K. in the end, and if it's not O.K., it's not the end." If you didn't get the interview, or didn't get the job, it's not the end of the world and it's not the end of your search. Thomas Edison tried more than 3,000 filaments when he was inventing the light bulb. He didn't give up. He knew that every failure brought him one step closer to success. If you don't get a job that you apply for, be glad you got that one out of the way, as you are now closer than before to landing the job that's out there for you.

There is a job out there for you. You're going to find something and it's going to be wonderful. You're going to find the job you've been looking for. You're going to find the job that uses your skills, fulfills your passions, and rewards you appropriately. Or maybe it will meet only one or two of those needs. So you know what that means. While you work, you keep working your network, work on finding the better opportunity. Work on work.

TAKE CONTROL

Finding a job, finding a better job, finding the next job is going to be part of what you do for the rest of your working life. Since jobs are no longer permanent, you are going to forever be in job-search mode, even when you're employed. That may be disheartening, but it's a fact of life today. If you're employed, your job search might simply mean being alert and sensitive to what opportunities are out there. If you're not employed, you'll be more active in your search, but know that you are always going to be on the lookout for your next opportunity. You know what it's like to be unemployed; you may have experienced the free fall of being downsized. You don't want to be there again, so you need to keep your skills sharp and your eyes peeled so you don't miss that next opportunity. You have a skill that the majority of the workforce lacks. You know how to look for a job. You know how to take control of your future.

    You can do this.

    You're not going to be unemployed forever.

    You have the skills, you have the knowledge, and you have the drive.

    The time to put this all into action is now. Right now.

    Don't put it off, don't wait another minute.

    Someone's gonna get hired.

    It might as well be you.

APPENDIX—FAQ'S
. . . and not so FAQs

I've come to the conclusion that there is no question too bizarre for a jobseeker to worry about. Whether in the middle of the night, the middle of a coaching session or the middle of an interview, these nagging doubts steal in and erode your self-confidence. Here are several of the most frequently, and some not so frequently, asked questions that have been posed to me. Hopefully this will help prevent these worries from getting in your way. Whenever appropriate I've included how it turned out for the questioner.

SHOULD I DYE MY HAIR?

Does it make a difference if I let my hair grow out to its natural color (gray) in terms of pursuing a job or a graduate degree? I'm looking into a Masters in Education to go into teaching.

There are fewer stigmas about gray hair than previously. It's more about how you feel about it. If you feel more confident with darker hair, then dye. If you feel better about "this is me and there's nothing wrong with gray hair," then go with the natural color. There is still some prejudice related to age, but it can be overcome. Further, if you're talking about being a teacher, there is less prejudice than in other fields (e.g., IT or sales).

She did not dye her hair and got a job.

CAN MY RESUME EXCEED ONE PAGE?

I find it very unsettling when a recruiter tells me to "add this" or "add that" to my resume to satisfy their own agenda. To me, that is the purpose of the cover letter, which should lead to a phone conversation, then an interview and, ultimately the job. I don't want to be at odds with these recruiters. I would like to keep my resume to one page, and it's already busting out at the margins. Am I being inflexible?

A one-page resume, in this digital age, is no longer a hard and fast rule; just so long as what you're being asked to add is factual and not "enhancement" (lies). Many recruiters actually prefer a shorter, to-the-point cover letter, so it's okay to put more in the resume. The exception to this is if the position for which you are applying involves writing. Then your cover letter serves as your writing sample. Brevity may not be the goal here, but still make sure that your cover letter and your resume are well written, contain only the most relevant information, and are no longer than need be.

One thing I recommend when your resume does spill onto a second page: don't feel that you need to fill that second page. I think it shows good judgment and discretion if you don't. Just add the pertinent information.

Anyone with more than 10 years in the workforce has a right to go to a second page. Twenty years? Absolutely. Less than 10? Consider editing.

He did not "enhance" his resume and did secure the interview.

SHOULD I REAPPLY?

I applied for a sales position with my current employer (a retail outlet) that is a better position than the one I currently have. I was told that the position was being filled internally. I know the other person who is interested in the position and I get along well with her. But two weeks later I saw the job listed on one of the big job boards. Should I reapply? Should I ask my boss what's going on? I don't want to jeopardize my relationship with my co-worker or my boss.

Just because the job is listed doesn't mean they're going to fill it. Not if the position doesn't carry much value in the eyes of the store management. Your concerns about store politics and relations with other staff members are valid. These are the kind of things that tend to get someone fired more often than poor performance on the job. And while the better position may sound good in a vacuum, in the current environment (both store and economy) it may not be the best move to make. Since the store has done without a full-timer in the position for so long, it would be easy to cut this position if things don't turn around quickly. You can test the waters gently by letting management know that you would still be interested, but I wouldn't push this too much or too hard right now. So long as they know you're interested, that may be enough for now. Proceed, but with caution.

The organization never filled the position and she kept her job.

WHAT IF I'M ASKED TO COMPLETE
A WAIVER FOR A REFERENCE CHECK?

I'm being considered for a position and they are asking me to complete an "Inquiry Release for Employment Consideration" form. I don't mind giving them my Social Security number, but I am reluctant to give them my full date of birth. Would you please let me know if it's something that you feel I should give them regardless of whether I like doing it or not?

Asking you to sign a release is customary. In fact it's a good sign, as it means they are serious and will be checking references. According to the letter of the law, they are in violation for asking you for your date of birth prior to making an offer. The possibility of age discrimination rears its ugly head. All that being said, if they have your Social Security number and are using the Internet, it wouldn't be impossible to find your date of birth anyway.

So, do you want to ask them why they need your date of birth and possibly make them think twice about making you an offer? Probably not the best idea if you like the company and would say yes if an offer were extended. Post-hire you might consider pointing out to them that asking for a date of birth prior to a formal (written) offer exposes them to risk of a lawsuit.

She gave them the information and got the job.

WHAT SHOULD I DO IF I'M ASKED
TO DO A PROJECT "ON SPEC"

At the conclusion of a third interview with a company, I was given a project to do "on spec," i.e., without any compensation. I was told that another interview would be scheduled at which a number of people with whom I would work (if hired) would be in attendance and I would be expected to make a 15-20 minute presentation on what I'd come up with. I was also told that a laptop and projector would be available, so I think they expect a PowerPoint deck too. Can they do this, I mean give me work to do without paying me? Who keeps what I come up with?

This is actually a good thing. It means they are quite interested in you. This is not a scam to get your efforts for free. Think of it from their point of view. They are interested enough in you that they are treating you as a member of the staff before you have been hired. They will be investing a lot of people hours in you (when the meeting is convened).

If you are not hired but they would like to keep your presentation, you are entitled to negotiate compensation for your work.

They loved her presentation but opted to fill the position internally.

HOW DO I DETERMINE WHAT TO
DO NEXT IF CAREER SHIFTING?

I'm thinking of changing careers after 15 years in one field. I'm willing to try anything, but how can I determine what else I might be suited for and like doing? I need to maintain a steady stream of income, so just going back to school is not an option.

There are lots of questions in this book that can help you figure this out.

Make a list of the things you have done in your professional life of which you are the most proud. Not everything that you're proud of; the things you're most proud of. You may want to include volunteer positions you've held.

This isn't easy. Take your time with it. Make a list of 25-30 things. Then edit it down to the top 7-10. You need to exercise discipline. That will serve you well in your search. Part of what may be holding you back is too open an approach. You are open and willing to try anything. One of the keys to success is figuring out which things to remain open to and which are sapping your energy and attention.

Part of figuring out what to do next is figuring out what has given you the greatest joy, pride, distinction and sense of accomplishment in the past. If you list everything you've ever done, then they will all have equal (and less) weight. This will not serve you in identifying a path.

He worked through the process and successfully changed careers.

HOW CAN I NETWORK WITH PEOPLE I'VE ALREADY REACHED OUT TO?

I feel so needy when I'm reaching out to people for the second or third time. I start to feel like a real imposition on their time and worry that maybe they'll start blocking or ignoring my calls. What can I do?

A great way to network is to send out notices about jobs to other people who are looking. Send postings about positions for which you are not suited. It costs you nothing and can generate lots of good karma. Plus it is a great way to keep in touch with people in your network who you haven't been in contact with. This works with people who are employed as well as those out of work. You're letting them know that you're active and not just waiting around for someone to offer you something. You are demonstrating what Stephen Covey calls an "abundance mentality." You are sharing what you can even if it may not directly benefit you. This is a good trait to show people and one that you can refer back to in interviews when you are asked to demonstrate how or why you consider yourself a team player.

Lots of people say they don't like to repeatedly call contacts in their network; they're afraid that the people they're calling will think they are asking for something. A job, a lead, another contact. Instead, give them something. Imagine if you gave someone else a lead that got him or her a job. You know that that person will work doubly hard to help you find one given the opportunity. If you don't have leads to send, consider sending articles that you think might interest some of your currently employed network contacts. You have more time to search the Internet than they do, and it's a great way to keep in touch.

She kept networking and secured a fulfilling part-time job.

IS IT UNETHICAL TO HARVEST E-MAILS?

I recently got an e-mail from a friend and there were lots of other people in the "To:" section. I could tell, from the e-mail addresses, that a couple of these were with companies on my target list. Is it okay to reach out to them?

Many of us have gotten e-mails from a friend or contact that has also been sent to dozens of other people. Look at all those interesting names in the "To:" or "CC:" section. From their e-mail addresses you can tell that many are working at companies you've targeted and would love to get a warm referral. Well now you can.

This is referred to as harvesting e-mails. Suppose that you are networking and trying to find someone who works in a certain industry or organization. When you get a message forwarded to you that has lots of people visible in the addressee boxes, this can be a way to make those contacts. All you have to do now is turn them into third circle contacts in your network. You know someone who knows someone who works in that organization that you'd love to be a part of. You can research the organization more easily because now you have the web address, and you even have a contact within the organization.

"But how can I network with someone I don't know?" you ask.

"All I have is their e-mail address." Your first step is to go back to the person who sent the e-mail. The sender has a relationship with the person at the target company. Ask the sender to help you reach out to the person with whom you'd like to speak. When you contact the person you can reference the sender of the e-mail.

When you send large distribution e-mails, protect your contacts by using "BCC:" You don't know who on your distribution is looking to harvest e-mails. And you can't guarantee that everyone on the list will check with you before contacting someone in your network. It doesn't do you any good to be the person who left the door open.

Protect the e-mail addresses of the people you know. Be gracious in treating the e-mails of people you want to know.

Sometimes you'll get the name of a person at an organization (from a newspaper article or such) but don't have their e-mail address. By harvesting you can get the company's e-mail protocol and send an e-mail directly to the person you are trying to reach. When you reach out to that person, reference the article in which you heard or read about them. You are not stalking the person and they may actually be flattered that you saw them in the paper or heard them on the radio.

It's not unethical, as some might tell you. It's networking, and it's necessary. All's fair in love, war and job-hunting.

The person checked with the sender of the e-mail before contacting people and made connections at target companies.

SHOULD I FOLLOW UP WITH AN EMPLOYER TO FIND OUT WHY I WAS TURNED DOWN FOR A POSITION?

I was recently turned down for a position. I knew it was a long shot, but having been out of work so long, I've been expanding my search. Is it worth following up with them to find out why? I expect they'll say that I have no industry experience. But if I'm doing something wrong in my interviews, I'd like to know.

You certainly should follow up with the employer to see if you can find out why you didn't get the job. They'll probably fall back on the old "We found a more qualified candidate," but at least they'll know you were sincere. And you might get some valuable feedback about your interviewing presentation. It also gives you one more chance to network with this contact, saying that you appreciate their consideration and would further appreciate their passing your resume on to anyone else whom they know who might be looking for someone with your skills. Do what you can to turn this rejection into a referral.

He followed up with the company but their policy prevented the recruiter from providing any additional information.

WHAT DO I DO WHEN I FEEL LIKE I'M LETTING MY FAMILY DOWN?

I was just turned down for another job. I didn't even really want this job, but I need a job. My husband is getting really tense with my being out of work. I'm tired of the looks I get from my teenage daughter when she gets home from school and I am there. I feel like I'm letting them down.

This is a real tough one. You're not letting anyone down unless you stay down. When you lose a job or don't have a job, you often feel like you're letting people down. Your spouse, your kids, your extended family and, of course, yourself.

Losing a job or not getting a job you've applied for is part of the employment cycle. Virtually everyone finds themselves out of work or in an uncertain situation at some point during the 40 to 50 years that we're part of the workforce. Being unemployed is hard. Finding work is hard. Keeping a job is hard. Remaining productive on the job when you're terrified you might lose it is nerve-wracking. No one said work is easy. At times, and for some people, it may be enjoyable, even fun. But that doesn't make it easy. I love my job, but it isn't easy. I have to work at it and I have to work on myself to keep working at it. Success was once defined as getting up one time more than you get knocked down. You don't have the luxury of staying down. Go to your SN (Support Network) before your start your next round of networking or interviewing. Get reinvigorated. If you are unemployed, you are not unique. You have lots of company, and the fact that you didn't get the job may not even have anything to do with the way you interviewed. There are many other factors at play.

Put this one behind you. Take from the experience what you can and move on. It's okay to get knocked down once in a while. It's okay to acknowledge the pain. Just don't set out the teacups for a pity party. Move on and don't stay down.

She resumed networking and interviewing and got a job.

WHAT'S YOUR TAKE REGARDING A RECRUITER ASKING IF IT IS OKAY TO CHANGE AN END DATE ON THE RESUME?

In the fall of 2008, I had a recruiter ask me to change my end date for a position from December 2007 to January 2008. The recruiter talked me into agreeing to list January 2008 as the exit date, insinuating that it looked better if I hadn't been out of work for over a year. I told her that if a company had a concern regarding how long I had been out of work, then I would not want to work for that company. She said that this request had come from her account manager and was apparently a preemptive request, and was not necessarily a reflection on the client.

I am against changing your end date. If a prospective employer were to check your dates of employment with your former employers and found discrepancies, they will eliminate you from consideration based on falsification of application. On most applications there is a disclaimer stating that the information is accurate and factual to the best of your knowledge. Any intentional falsification of information or misstatement can be grounds for termination.

I can understand the recruiter's desire to make it look like you have been out of work less time, but this is a very slippery slope.

He did not change the dates and the recruiter did not submit him for the position.

SHOULD I LIST MONTH AND YEAR IN THE
DATES OF EMPLOYMENT ON MY RESUME?

I had a recruiter suggest that I put December 2007 as my end date instead of 2007 as a way to eliminate getting asked when in 2007 I left. If I do include the month, then should I include the month for all other dates for all listed positions?

Regarding month/year, it doesn't hurt to do this for the last position and if you do, then consistency throughout the resume is best, but not mandatory. If you were at a position for 12 years, do they really care which month you started? Month/year is usually used for short-term assignments.

SHOULD MY RESUME HAVE AN "OBJECTIVE"
OR A "SUMMARY"?

I've heard differing theories about what to have at the top of my resume. Some say an objective while others say a summary or profile. Which is best?

This depends very often on the stage of your career. Usually newer entrants to the workforce will opt for an objective. It's a good idea to let the recruiter or hiring manager know what it is you hope to accomplish in your career, and more important, what you can do for the company when hired.

More experienced jobseekers will find that a summary of their professional experience is a more effective lead-in to the resume. If you are making a mid-career shift, then an objective may be a better way to make clear to the reader why you are applying.

Objectives used to be the preferred beginning to a resume but that has changed as people pursue multiple careers over the course of their work life. When crafting an objective, remember it's not all about you. A good objective doesn't simply outline the benefit to you if you are hired. ("I am seeking a position that will further develop my sales and marketing skills.") Better objectives convey to the reader the benefit to the company of selecting you. ("I am seeking an opportunity to use my sales and marketing skills

186

to help the department and organization achieve and exceed its goals.") Use this as an opportunity to sell the benefit of hiring you.

HOW LONG SHOULD MY "ELEVATOR PITCH" BE?

Most people feel that your elevator pitch, or introductory statement, should be in the 15-30 second range. Recently, I've heard that the "two minute drill," a more extended pitch, may be more important than an elevator spiel. Way back when (in the '90s), before everyone was crafting 15-second elevator pitches, the two-minute introductory statement was common. I think it was during the dot-com era that two minutes shrank to 15 seconds. Rather than defend one versus the other, you must have both. Because if someone is intrigued by your 15-30-second elevator pitch and asks for more information, you must have something prepared to say.

WHAT DO I DO IF THEY ASK ME ABOUT SALARY?

Do your homework

1. Check the Internet sites that list average starting salaries.

2. Go to other job boards and see if you can find comparable postings that include a starting salary.

3. Use a range instead of a hard figure. They will likely use the bottom of the range when negotiating your starting salary.

4. What do you need to feel good about this job? What do you need to make ends meet? What you need does not affect what they will pay, but it's good for you to know your lowest acceptable figure as well as your desired salary.

5. If you have contacts in your network familiar with the market, ask them what they think the job might pay.

WHY IS THE HIRING PROCESS SO INEFFICIENT?

Since 80% of all jobs are filled by being known in advance or knowing those who point you to opportunities, does this process mean that the free market is grossly inefficient, i.e., more-qualified candidates will be hired only 20% of the time because the basis of networking is who you know, not what you know?

The sourcing and hiring process is inefficient, if only because too many recruiters fly by the seat of their pants instead of applying sound practices and metrics to what they are doing. They are the hamsters in the wheel.

But do not assume that the 80% who get hired through networking and contacts are not qualified. They most likely are, or they wouldn't have been referred in the first place, but as you point out, they may not be the most qualified. The pressure put on recruiters to fill positions quickly often results in compromises along the lines of another 80/20 rule. "Done is better than perfect." The recruiter may not have found the best candidate, but at least found one who meets enough of the requirements of the job to close the deal.

If most jobs are filled through networking, i.e., referrals from people we know or have worked with, this is one more argument for ongoing networking both while employed and unemployed.

INDEX

www.ingramcontent.com/pod-product-compliance
Lightning Source LLC
Chambersburg PA
CBHW060548210326
41519CB00014B/3393